THE GLASS HOUSE

POLITICS & MORALITY IN THE NATION'S CAPITAL

CONGRESSMAN
PAUL SIMON

ngressman from Illinois,
and publisher who has
lly acclaimed books, in-
merican and *The Once*

Every American is fascinated by headlines that expose the personal weaknesses of public officials, especially those so called "capitol sins" that take place behind closed doors. But Congressman Paul Simon asks, "What really *is* political morality?" Does it have to do with a senator's or congressman's private life, or how he or she exercises power for the public service—or disservice—of others?

Unafraid to be specific, or even to reveal his own failings as an elected official, Simon contrasts, for instance, the lethargic response of many public figures to hunger and the nuclear threat with their often self-righteous trumpeting of marginal issues, and shows that a politician's struggle to do what is right and just is a complex issue, made up of hundreds of important choices that never make headlines and are not easy—either for the conscientious public official or for the conscientious citizens who select, or reject, their leaders.

Simon tackles such issues with moral implications as honesty, time, money, campaigning, "religion", relations with the media, personal behavior versus public service, abortion, lobbying, self-restraint ver leadership, the two-party system, and the "god" public opinion. He provides an unsparing look at real criteria for political morality as actually m: ifested in some of our nation's most powerful n and women, and the people who support them—ignore them.

(continued on back flap)

The Glass House

THE
GLASS HOUSE

☆ POLITICS AND MORALITY
IN THE NATION'S CAPITAL

PAUL SIMON

CONTINUUM ☆ NEW YORK

1984
The Continuum Publishing Company
370 Lexington Avenue, New York, N.Y. 10017

Library of Congress Cataloging in Publication Data
Simon, Paul, 1928–
   The glass house.
   Includes bibliographical references.
   1. Legislators—United States. 2. United States.
Congress—Ethics. 3. Political ethics. I. Title.
JK1051.S57   1984   328.73'073   83-26277
ISBN 0-8264-0246-1

To the memory of Paul H. Douglas
whose struggle in the political arena
reflected ethical conduct at its finest.

Contents

Introduction

As a public official striving toward desirable goals, I am faced with a series of dilemmas. This book offers a look at that complex quest.

The assumption from which I start these reflections is that there are morally preferred options, and that it is the responsibility of humanity and of government to strive toward the good, no matter how erratic and tortuous that path may be.

I make one more assumption: what appears to be obvious is not necessarily so. By oversimplifying the quest for good, we make a noble goal less achievable. By equating personal morality with public morality, we sometimes do harm to the latter.

In some pseudosophisticated circles it is assserted that there are no morally preferred options—often a defense for inaction, or a parroting by the gullible of a judgment someone has conveyed as wisdom.

There are goals and options on which most people can agree: freedom is better than tyranny, help for the handicapped better than neglect, control of smallpox better than its spread, ample food supply better than famine, peace better than war. A list of clearly preferred options where moral choices are involved would be lengthy.

But how we can preserve freedom, help the handicapped, stop smallpox, provide for an adequate food supply, avoid war—these questions of method and means—involve complex decisions. Oversimplification can hurt the causes we espouse.

I have spent fourteen years in the General Assembly of Illinois, four years as lieutenant governor, and nine years in the U.S. House of Representatives. From the mail I have received over those years and the comments I have heard, I gather that most people assume government officials face clear-cut choices between good and evil. I wish that were so. I hope this book helps the public understand the kind of grappling with decisions faced by officeholders.

I am grateful to many for their comments and suggestions, including colleagues in the House and Senate, and the following who helped on the manuscript in specific ways: my wife, Jeanne; my favorite two college sudents, my daughter Sheila and my son Martin; my brother Arthur Simon, executive director of Bread for the World; Berkley Bedell and Anthony Beilenson, my colleagues in the House; Bonnie Black, author of *The Somewhere Child*; William Byron, S.J., president of The Catholic University of America; Gene Callahan, administrative assistant to Senator Alan J. Dixon; David Carle, Ray Johnsen, Job Bob Pierce, and Gerald and Ellen Sinclair, who have been associated with me in public life; Robert Cornell, Norbertine priest and former member of the House; James Ford, chaplain of the House; John Marty, future Minnesota political leader; Martin Marty, theologian and historian; William E. Leuchtenberg, Franklin D. Roosevelt scholar and University of North Carolina professor; Patricia O'Brien, reporter and columnist for the Knight-Ridder newspapers; Tom F. Thompson, editor of *The Florida Skeptic*; Judith Wagner, House staff leader for the handicapped; and James Wall, editor of *The Christian Century*. Jay Willer helped with ideas and footnotes. Victorine Coupling typed and retyped the manuscript, patiently. Jeannette Hopkins has now braved editing my third book. Michael Leach of Crossroad/Continuum, my publisher, always has been encouraging. All have enriched the final product, but are not responsible for the errors of judgment the reader may detect.

Those of us in political life live in a glass house. The spotlight shines on it and what you see is not always pleasant. This book is an attempt to tell you something more about those of us in that glass house, about the struggles we go through, or should go through.

Paul Simon

The Cast of Characters

We have met the enemy and he is us.
—cartoonist Walt Kelly[1]

The louder he talked of his honor the faster we counted our spoons.
—Ralph Waldo Emerson[2]

There are two things you should not see made: laws and sausage.
—old American saying

Politics affects all citizens. Literally everyone is involved, either actively or passively; but it is the leaders or nominal leaders who can, through the power of their vote or the power of their decisions, create a world with more hope or less hope, more justice or less justice, and literally have the power to destroy civilization. Legislators are leaders by definition, and few get to their position without a willingness to take some risks. We are people with strong convictions, strong opinions, strong ambitions, strong passions, and more power than most. We have volunteered to take more pressure than most citizens do, as well as more criticism and more praise. Each member of Congress has the opportunity to display strengths and weaknesses, and those who follow the congressional scene closely see both in each of us. Because of the spotlight on House and Senate membership, our virtues and vices are magnified. We are in one of the few professions in which a person is required to stand up and publicly say, "I can do a better job than my opponent." That takes a special kind of ego.

The public image of those on the Washington scene is much like a TV crime show or an old-fashioned western, with "good guys" and "bad guys"—clearly defined. That simplistic view is not accurate in your community, and it is also far from accurate in Washington.

There is *some* truth to Lord Acton's famous quote: "Power tends to corrupt, and absolute power corrupts absolutely."[3] All government power needs checks. No individual and no government should be given unrestrained authority. But Acton's statement can easily get distorted into two falsehoods. The first is that it is possible and in the public interest to have an absence of power. Generally, a power vacuum cannot be created, and where free systems have had drifting, ineffective government, the result has not been ennobling. Poland's often unhappy history includes such a period, when there was no concentration of power and all members of the Polish Diet were required to give their approval before any action could be taken. The resulting chaos helped to bring down the government. Second, Acton's maxim has been interpreted by some to suggest that those who avoid power are somehow more virtuous. Although this may comfort those without power, an unwillingness to use power, and the opportunites for good that come with it, is not a moral stance. The consciences of those unwilling to assume responsibility should not be so easily salved. The souls of those with leadership potential who avoid power are as tainted as those who abuse it. That is the lesson of the biblical story of the man who entrusted responsibility to his servants while he went on a journey.[4] Those who used their talents were rewarded. The man who failed to use his talent was punished.

Lord Acton's statement appears in a variety of forms. Poet William Blake wrote:

> The strongest poison ever known
> Came from Caesar's laurel crown.[5]

Poison it sometimes is. But the public should know who the modern Caesars are and what the real nature of the struggle is.

Richard Neuhaus made an observation more astute than Lord Acton's: "Politics is concerned with the distribution and exercise of power. The goal is not to get beyond . . . the use of power but to make [it] as apparent, as accessible and as just as possible."[6]

The difficulties faced in the exercise of power are apparent daily in Congress.

A small, informal meeting had just ended. It involved House and Senate members who gather once a month to discuss the food and overpopulation problems facing poor countries. As I left and walked down the corridor of that graceless hulk called the Rayburn Building, I talked with Representative Millicent Fenwick, a pipe-smoking Republican, who in 1982 lost a race for the Senate. The citizens of the Fifth Congressional District of New Jersey elected her to the House at the age of sixty-four. "You know," she said as we walked along, "I come away from a meeting like this tremendously impressed by the quality of the membership of Congress. But somehow the end product does not seem to reflect that quality."

Both of her observations are valid. New Jersey Senator Nicholas Brady, a businessman appointed to fill the seat left vacant by the resignation of Senator Harrison Williams in the wake of the Abscam scandal, noted the same: "The people here are of a higher caliber than I imagined in my fondest dreams. But the place doesn't work very well. It's very frustrating."[7]

It would not make news—or sell books—to describe the membership of Congress as much above the quality the public perceives, and some would add, deserves. The truly great champion of high ethical standards, Senator Paul Douglas, told me a few months before his death that the Senate "today is a much finer body than when I served in it." He referred not to ability but to ethical standards. In 1977, ninety-two-year-old historian Will Durant said that the intellectual level of Congress is "as high as at any time in our history, except the first generation of the Founding Fathers, and really we were ruled by an aristocracy then."[8] Although we now revere the Founding Fathers (a phrase given us by Warren G. Harding), a critic of one of the first congresses said it was "a prostitution of the name of Government to apply it to such a vagabond, strolling, contemptible crew as

Congress."⁹ One of the harshest critics of politicians in U.S. history, muckraking journalist Lincoln Steffens, wrote in his autobiography: "The ethics and morals of politics are higher than those of business."¹⁰ The evolving change in ethical standards can be seen in the newspapers almost daily and in examples through the years.

In 1956 the courts convicted Representative Thomas J. Lane of Massachusetts of evading $38,542 in income taxes. During his fifteenth year in Congress he served five months in a federal penitentiary. After his release, his colleages welcomed him back to the halls of Congress. Two months later the voters of his Massachusetts constituency reelected him. Today he would not be able to return to Congress and he probably would not be reelected.

Daniel Webster often has been held up as a heroic example of a great nineteenth-century senator. But if a United States senator today openly demanded money from the railroads for support of legislation, as Webster did, that solon would quickly lose his or her seat.

Representative James Garfield accepted a gift of stock from a company seeking legislative favors, and he neither found his career ruined (he later became president) nor faced censure in the House.

Members of the House and Senate share responsibility for the bad public image because it is politically popular to denounce Congress, to say by implication, "I am a good guy, but watch out for these other rascals." Robert Cornell, a Roman Catholic priest who served in the House from Wisconsion, recalls:

> Some members are responsible for the low esteem in which Congress is held by the public because [they] campaign against Congress. I recall that during my reelection campaign in 1976 I defended Congress at a fundraiser and my campaign manager, a Capitol Hill veteran . . . remarked: "That was a good speech, but I wouldn't have given it. That won't win you votes."
> The first speech I gave after leaving office was at a weekly breakfast of a retired businessmen's club. . . . I emphasized that miscreant members of Congress get the news coverage, not the many fine, dedicated, hardworking people I came to

know. I observed that most of them compared very well with the members of the religious order to which I belong. Nevertheless the first questioner remarked: "I don't care what you say; they're all crooks."[11]

There are some in Congress who are venal, but my guess is that they are few. Venality is markedly rarer in Congress than it was in the General Assembly of Illinois during my days there.[12] That body and most state legislatures have improved in the last twenty years. Others can speak more knowledgeably than I about local government, though one Massachusetts legislator once noted that Diogenes went through the Boston City Council seeking an honest man and came out without his lantern.[13] Nevertheless, it is my impression that the level of integrity in local government has risen, just as it has in the state and federal governments. The few members of Congress who may be corrupt don't advertise who they are. I have a few suspicions, as do other members, as do reporters, but all of us could be wrong in our guesses. What is certain is that the outright corrupt—those who accept direct bribes—are a small minority.

Before being elected to Congress in 1974, I had visited Washington often. But I did not expect the overall quality that I found when I became a member. Although I had been in public life before coming to Congress, I had absorbed enough of the bad news to believe that Capitol Hill lawmakers would not be appreciably more able than those I had observed in state legislative bodies. I misjudged. For every old and crotchety member there are several who are old and wise. For every young and arrogant member there are several who are young and eager to learn. For every ethically devious member there are many who take their responsibilities seriously.

Sometimes the collective performance of 435 House members or 100 senators is enough to send you home at night discouraged. But the problems are not going to be solved by simplistic images. The moral dilemmas House and Senate members face are not as clear-cut as, for example, the proper response to a bribe, but rather relate to a host of issues and problems far more subtle, far more complex.

A few years ago a casual conversation about former Representative Wilbur Mills of Arkansas would not have reflected well
on him. When he publicly squired striptease artist Fannie Fox
around the country, headline writers and comedians had a field
day. One of the most respected members of Congress until this
episode, Mills had been a dominant force in tax legislation for
many years. Foreign countries had sent representatives to Mills
rather than to the White House to discuss export matters. But
the nation roared with laughter as he appeared on a Boston
burlesque stage to take a bow. Once considered presidential material, he now looked like a fool. He publicly admitted his problem: alchoholism.

I've heard many jokes about Mills from people who have never
met him. But there's an unknown side to him. When a friend of
mine developed a serious drinking problem, Wilbur Mills went
out of his way to help him. My friend is only one of many people
Wilbur Mills has helped. I do not defend Mills's capers, but I
have come to know the other side of the story.

Similarly, Richard Nixon, a former member of the House of
Representatives and the Senate who fell from grace at about the
same time as Mills, will not receive a hero's treatment in the
history books, but my guess is that history will be somewhat
kinder to him than current opinion for the forward steps taken
in our relations with China and the Soviet Union under his leadership. Richard Nixon's mistakes should not prevent our listening to him, for example, when he suggests that if we do not want
to destroy the world we ought to be doing more to get along
with the other great superpower. The public and officeholders
should not be so eager to cast people as villains that we do not
at least listen to them.

Wilbur Mills was not the first chairman of the House Ways
and Means Committee whose personal conduct caused national
controversy. John Randolph of Roanoke, Virginia (1773–1833)—
colorful, unpredictable, and powerful—got an early start on his
controversial career. William and Mary College expelled him
when he fought a duel over the proper pronunciation of a word.

A heavy drinker even as a youth, he had an unusual appearance, tall with extremely thin legs and unable to grow a beard to cover his florid face. He never married, and when some of his bitter foes made light of his high-pitched voice and charged him with impotency (which he did not deny), he responded: "You pride yourself upon an animal faculty, in . . . [which] the jackass [is] infinitely your superior!"[14] He called himself Citizen Randolph and called others virtually every name in the book; public officials feared him. Despite his poor health, he could stand on the floor of the House for two or three hours at a time piercing the air with his high voice, bitter denunciations, and gifted oratory. Before he was thirty he emerged as the Republican (Jeffersonian) leader of the House. Jefferson, Randolph's cousin and his bitter enemy, later tried three times to have Randolph defeated. Another cousin who differed with Randolph received permanent scars from Randolph's whip. When Andrew Jackson became president, Randolph retired from the House, and Jackson named him ambassador to Russia. The Senate unanimously confirmed him, despite public knowledge of his addiction to both alcohol and opium. He died in Philadelphia on May 24, 1833, with a whip in his hand. A few days before his death, Randolph's physician told his weak patient that he would like to bring in another doctor for consultation. Randolph declined, saying, "In a multitude of counsel there is confusion. . . . The patient may die while the doctors are staring at each other."[15]

Not a typical member of Congress, John Randolph nevertheless entered congressional halls as another of a series of strong personalities who determine the nation's future.

And sometimes the "good guys" aren't so good.

Near the turn of the century in England, Joseph Burgess, a Labour candidate for a seat in the House of Commons, refused to compromise on an issue long since obscure. Because of his intransigence, the victory went to the opposition. Burgess, editor of a publication called *Workman's Times*, apparently expected to be hailed for his refusal. But one of those who criticized him was George Bernard Shaw, who commented:

> When I think of my own character, smirched with compro-
> mise, rotted with opportunism, mildewed by expediency—
> dragged through the mud of borough council and Battersea
> elections, stretched out of shape with wire-pulling, putri-
> fied by permeation, worn out by twenty-five years pushing
> to gain an inch here, or straining to stem a backrush, I do
> think Joe might have put up with just a speck or two on
> those white robes of his for the sake of the millions of
> poor devils who cannot afford any character at all because
> they have no friend in Parliament. Oh, these moral dandies,
> these spiritual toffs, these superior persons. Who is Joe,
> anyhow, that he should not risk his soul occasionally like
> the rest of us?[16]

Shaw's derision of the purist is well placed. Former Representative Joseph Fisher of Virginia described the process of compromise well when he paraphrased Shakespeare: "The best is
sometimes the enemy of the good, and the bad must sometimes
be chosen rather than the terrible."[17]

The first time I ran for public office, for state representative,
I met a woman in Granite City, Illinois, who said that she had
read what I stood for and applauded my stands. "And I'm going
to pray for your election," she said. "But I'm not going to vote
because I don't believe in getting mixed up in politics." Those
who remain so certain that only they are right, and those who
remain inflexible about a particular position, unwilling to make
an honorable compromise to advance toward a goal, contribute
little to bringing our society closer to the ends they profess to
espouse.

That is not the only failing of the "good guys." They make
mistakes; they are sometimes petty. It's nice to have heroes, but
real heroes are also real people.

A while ago Representative Paul Findley of Illinois introduced
an amendment to a military assistance bill that would have given
the president a little more flexibility in dealing with the sensitive
Greek-Turkish situation. The amendment came to a vote un-
expectedly and as the voting proceeded, members gathered in
small knots on the floor to discuss it. There is a feeling of kinship
for Greece in Congress because that nation threw off its dicta-

torship in 1974, because so much of our democratic heritage comes from the ancient Greeks, and because of the political reality that there are a great many more Greeks than Turks living in the United States. As four of us discussed the matter—Representatives Jonathan Bingham and Stephen Solarz, both of New York, a nationally prominent and respected congressman, and I—Bingham said, "The politically advantageous vote is to vote against Findley. The responsible vote is to vote with him." I happened to disagree with that assessment, but before I could comment the nationally prominent legislator smiled and said, "I think I'll cast an irresponsible vote." There are soft spots in the armor of even the best.

By some standards, I'm one of the "good guys" in the House. I disclose my income, assets, and liabilities in detail and have done so longer than any other public official in the nation. I generally support the types of things that Common Cause and the League of Women Voters favor; columnist Jack Anderson in a moment of generosity once listed me as one of the "best" members of Congress; and even most of the Republican newspapers in my district and state have supported me, a Democrat. But I could point out bad votes I've cast, though I thought they were good at the time.

One night, for example, the House had a debate on the defense budget. I then served on the Budget Committee's Task Force, which deals with defense matters. The House voted $4 billion more than we had approved, $4 billion not needed. With so many really pressing needs in the nation, I was irritated to see the Pentagon supporters swing the House over to that extra $4 billion. A few minutes later, a proposal for $500 million for additional bonuses for World War I veterans came up. It had not been cleared through the Veterans Committee, and we already had a hefty deficit. World War I veterans and their widows need greater help from the federal government, but doing it on the spur of the moment with an amendment on the floor, without knowing the full implications or any details, was not sensible. So I voted no. But the more I thought about that extra $4 billion wasted on defense, and knowing that this vote would be listed by veterans' organizations and senior citizens, I said to myself,

"If we can spend money foolishly on that, why not spend one-eighth of the amount on these poor old people." I changed my vote to yes. It was probably a bad vote. I cast it when irritated. Whatever program we devise ought to emerge after careful study.

From Wilbur Mills to John Randolph, from Richard Nixon to those representing you in the House and Senate, you will find the cast of characters is in many ways similar to those in the community where you live. We are similar in occupation, although members of Congress are more likely to be lawyers (261 of 535 are lawyers); we are farmers and journalists, physicians and teachers, just as you are. We have had house painters, plumbers, and pharmacists in our midst, almost any occupation you can name.

But in some ways we are unrepresentative. Two of the senators and twenty-one of the House members are women. Twenty House members are black, but there are none in the Senate. In the House there are nine Hispanics, but none in the Senate. All three groups are underrepresented, but their numbers are growing.

We are more likely to announce our religious affiliation than is the public at large. Roman Catholicism, the largest numerical religious group in the country, with fifty million followers, can also claim the largest number in Congress with 141. Episcopalians are the most heavily represented relative to membership numbers of the major denominations, with sixty-one members for three million Episcopalians. Baptists have forty-six members for thirty million, and Lutherans twenty-five for nine million. Presbyterians have fifty-four members for their ranks of four million, and Jews have thirty-eight for six million.

Diversity of background, gregariousness—these and other qualities fit the nation's legislators and legislative body. But that is only part of the story. Two thousand years ago Plutarch described what for many is the essence of politics:

> They are wrong who think that politics is like an ocean voyage or a military campaign, something to be done with some particular end in view, something which leaves off as soon as that end is reached. It is not a public chore, to be got over with. It is a way of life. It is the life of a domesticated political

and social creature who is born with a love for public life, with a desire for honor, with a feeling for his fellows . . .[18]

That description fits many, but not all, in public life. There are no generalities that are universally applicable. The quest for good in public life is complex, and so is the cast of characters.

☆ 2 ☆

Allen Howe
and the People of Utah

Nowhere are prejudices more mistaken for truth, passion for
reason, and invective for documentation than in politics. That
is a realm, peopled only by villains or heroes, in which everything is black or white and gray is a forbidden color.
—John Mason Brown[1]

A great deal of cant, hypocrisy and sensationalism is being
heard about the so-called "Washington sex scandal" and the
principal victim so far is the unfortunate Representative Allen
T. Howe of Utah.
—Tom Wicker, *New York Times*
June 22, 1976[2]

Desire is a wild beast, and passion perverts the minds of rulers
even when they are the best of men.
—Aristotle[3]

Representative Allen Howe seemed fairly inconspicuous in
the sometimes brash and outspoken freshman congressional class of 1975. Conscientious and able but not noisy, he
gained the respect of his colleagues on both sides of the aisle.
At the age of forty-eight, paying attention to the special needs
of his Utah constituency, he seemed destined for a long career
in the House, if he wanted one. There may have been rumors
about marital difficulties, but whenever there are 435 people
working together there are bound to be rumors (frequently un-
founded), particularly in such a divorce-prone occupation. If an

enterprising reporter had taken a poll asking House members for the twenty in their midst who might be destined for some type of sensational story, Howe would not have made the top twenty and probably would not have received any votes.

But the votes would have been miscast.

Utah, like other states, has not been immune to unfavorable headlines. In 1886, ten years before Utah became a state, Deputy U.S. Marshal Oscar C. Vandercook went to Utah to crack down on the practice of polygamy, which violated new federal statutes. Before heading into a remote area of Utah, he visited a Salt Lake City brothel. The madam who ran it, as it was subsequently disclosed, had been paid to lure Vandercook into the place. The aim: to discredit the federal government's attempts to eliminate polygamy. Arrested on a warrant filed by B. Y. Hampton, a city license collector, the local courts ordered Vandercook to pay two hundred dollars and serve three months in jail. Vandercook appealed, charging entrapment. The federal courts reversed the conviction and ultimately Hampton spent a year in jail for his part in the conspiracy.

Whether this case has parallels to that of Representative Allen Howe is a matter of dispute, but not of legal dispute. On June 12, 1976, police arrested Howe for "soliciting sex acts for hire." Officers said that he had propositioned a policewoman posing as a prostitute. Howe, a Mormon and the father of five children, charged that he had been entrapped by political enemies, that he had been lured to the scene by a man who had asked him to attend a political gathering in the area. Howe was vague about the man's identity and the political gathering.

The arrest received added publicity because not many weeks earlier Elizabeth Ray had charged Representative Wayne Hays with keeping her on the payroll solely for sexual services she provided him. The Hays incident had erupted like a volcano in Washington and had led to his resignation from the House. Howe told the *Deseret News* of Salt Lake City: "An elected official's public and private standards should be equally high. I definitely do not believe that Hays's activity is all that typical or widespread in Congress."[4] That statement did not help Howe later.

Pressure mounted within the Utah Democratic party for Howe to remove himself as a candidate for reelection. With the election only four and one-half months off, the *Deseret News* (owned by the Latter-Day Saints) called for Howe to step down, saying it "could have a national cleansing effect." The newspaper added, "We are not drawing any conclusions about whether he is guilty or innocent of charges he propositioned two police decoys posing as prostitutes. . . . His plea that Utahans withhold judgment is in keeping with the long and wise tradition of presuming any accused person innocent until found guilty in a court of law."[5] There were, however, "larger and more compelling principles that point to a prompt resignation as being in the best interests of all concerned."

In the meantime, civil liberties groups and others protested the use of police decoys. Bruce Ennis of the New York Civil Liberties Union commented, "We think it's unseemly for the government to participate in the creation of criminal acts and then prosecute someone for joining in them. It's an inappropriate use of government resources in victimless crimes when they could be paying more attention to serious crimes."[6]

Howe decided to stay in the race. On July 23, 1976, a jury of three women and one man deliberated ninety-eight minutes and found him guilty of offering money for "the performance of sex acts for hire." Howe described the decision by the city court as "a disappointment" but said he would appeal the case and continue to seek reelection to Congress. His case went to the district court of Utah, where a jury of five men and three women deliberated less than thirty minutes before finding him guilty. Ten days later Howe announced again that he would stay in the race. He told reporters, "I have been deeply heartened by the support of new and old friends. After intensive examination of every factor of my situation I will stand on my record and continue seeking re-election. . . . It was a mistake, as I have said, for me to go to that area of Salt Lake City. But to err is human. I have said I have faith in the people of Utah and I believe that sincerely."

He added, "I have suffered political damage but believe I can win." The same day newspapers reported Howe was experiencing great difficulty in raising funds for his campaign. The day before he announced his decision to stay in the race, the *Salt Lake Tribune* had published a poll showing he had only 15 percent of the vote. To add to the congressman's complications, the president of the Church of Jesus Christ of Latter-Day Saints expressed regret at "the embarrassment" this had caused the Mormon church. "Church spokesmen" said that Howe might face excommunication. Utah is approximately 75 percent Mormon. Two weeks later Democratic leaders of Salt Lake County (87 percent of Howe's congressional district) met and announced that they were backing a write-in candidate, Daryl J. McCarty. That put three in the race: Howe, McCarty, and Republican Dan Marriott. The results on election day: Marriott, 128,011 (53 percent); Howe, 92,938 (39 percent) and McCarty, 18,559 (8 percent).

Had Allen Howe been in almost any other profession, his arrest would have gone almost unnoticed. We as a people are inconsistent in what we say about our leaders and what we demand of them. We believe, according to the polls, that a high percentage of them are corrupt and represent the less desirable elements in our society. Fathers and mothers would like to see their children become president of the United States, but a look of dismay will come to a parent's face if you say, "Maybe your child will grow up to become a politician." Those same fathers and mothers want their governmental leaders to represent the best in society in every way. Generally, such high standards are good. But a specific action or behavioral pattern that violates the norm can weigh too heavily. It can be something as trivial as Thomas E. Dewey's mustache (which alienated large numbers of American voters), or it can be a personal problem, such as Adlai E. Stevenson's divorce. "We'd like a family man as president," many people said during the two elections in which Stevenson sought the presidency.

Prior to Allen Howe's arrest, in the eight years Salt Lake City had its decoy program, police arrested 1,129 people. But only one of those arrests made national news, or even much local news. The week that Salt Lake City's police arrested Howe they arrested fourteen others (eleven men, three women) on the same charge of soliciting a prostitute. One of those arrested owned a car dealership, another served as a cashier at a bank, and the others' occupations varied from navigator to truck driver. But only one of those arrested that week made the news.

Eleven months after the Howe arrest, the Reverend Robert L. Bast, pastor of the Garfield Park Reformed Church of Grand

Rapids, Michigan, made national news when he pleaded no contest to a similar charge and the court fined him 110 dollars. The *Grand Rapids Press* reported that he "addressed his congregation the Sunday following the incident, saying he could not expect their forgiveness, but asked for their prayers. The consistory granted him a thirty-day leave of absence."[7] Within two weeks the church leaders voted to reinstate him.

One of the bulwarks of the Christian faith is the belief in the forgiveness of sins. There are those who would say that the leaders of the Garfield Park Reformed Church of Grand Rapids practiced forgiveness more fully than did the voters of the Second Congressional District of Utah.

It can hardly be insignificant that the only two cases like this to make the national news involved a congressman and a minister. Judging by the much greater attention given the congressman, it may be that our standards are higher for those holding public office than for the clergy.

There is, however, one major difference between the minister's action and the congressman's, and it points to an important trait in our national character. We tolerate mistakes when there is candor about them, but we do not tolerate what we perceive to be deception. Allen Howe protested his innocence, but the courts found him guilty. Whether guilty or not (a fact complicated by the use of the police-decoy approach), the real jury in the case of Allen Howe did not face him in court but in the voting booth. Their verdict has to be read: guilty. It is possible that if he had pleaded guilty, the voters of his district in Utah might have forgiven him. If they would do so for a preacher in Grand Rapids, they might for a politician in Utah.

In fact, there are many instances of voters forgiving an indiscretion or a serious mistake, but not forgiving a lack of candor. There are at least three examples of such candor in men who served with Howe in Congress: Representatives Frank Horton, Robert Leggett, and Wilbur Mills.

Mills acknowledged that he had been an alcoholic; he did not try to defend his conduct; he apologized for it. Mills sought and won reelection in 1974, and could have been reelected in 1976 had he run. He chose to retire. Horton, arrested and charged with a misdemeanor, driving while intoxicated, pleaded guilty (contrary to the advice of his lawyers); when a judge gave him a fine and suspended sentence, Horton said he ought to serve some time also, just as everyone else. He served one week in jail and became something of a local hero. Horton was reelected by a 65,502-vote majority. Leggett, charged with having fathered two children by a former aide, admitted it. Leggett won by a 726-vote majority. Horton, a Republican, and Leggett, a Democrat, were regarded as substantial members of the House, both making above-average contributions. Horton won in 1976 by 5,325 fewer votes than the majority he received in 1974. Leggett won in 1976 by 59,498 fewer votes than the majority he received in 1972; in 1974 he was not challenged.

Another colleague of Howe did not fare well. Representative Henry Helstoski, a New Jersey Democrat, suffered defeat when he sought his sixth term despite a federal indictment charging that he had received bribes to help illegal aliens remain in this country. It is doubtful that even an admission of guilt, or complete candor on his part, would have helped his cause. People are willing to understand accusations of drunken driving, alcoholism, and other charges involving a person's private life, but bribery is not a forgivable sin in the eyes of the voters, as it should not be.

The most dramatic example of candor and forgiveness on the national scene occurred during the presidential election of 1884. Grover Cleveland, son of a Presbyterian minister, became the Democratic nominee, and James G. Blaine, a former Speaker of the House and secretary of state, headed the Republican slate. Mud-slinging reached its heights in this campaign. Blaine, who had been involved in some questionable stock transactions, had scribbled on the back of a note to a Boston firm that handled his personal investments, "Burn this letter." It gave the Democrats their campaign song:

> Blaine, Blaine, James G. Blaine,
> The continental liar from the State of Maine,
> Burn this letter![8]

The Republicans located a Mrs. Maria Halpin, who claimed that Cleveland fathered her illegitimate son. Cleveland told his campaign manager that he intended to "tell the truth" and admitted with regret that he could have been the father. The Republicans then chanted:

> Ma! Ma! Where's my pa
> Gone to the White House.
> Ha! Ha! Ha![9]

An Illinois writer concluded: "We are told that Mr. Blaine has been delinquent in office but blameless in private life, while Mr. Cleveland has been a model of official integrity, but culpable in his personal relations. We should therefore elect Mr. Cleveland to the public office which he is so well qualified to fill, and remand Mr. Blaine to the private station which he is admirably fitted to adorn."[10]

The voters (then all male) were willing to forgive Cleveland his indiscretion and he became one of our better presidents. But what if Cleveland had denied the charge? No one knows the answer. What if Richard Nixon had admitted his guilt on the Watergate matter immediately and expressed great regret? What if Allen Howe had admitted guilt to the Utah charge and asked the forgiveness of the people of his district? We don't know the answers, but the lesson of American history from Grover Cleveland on down suggests that the public does not demand perfection from officials, but it does demand candor.

The questions posed by the Allen Howe case are complex. For example, if instead of talking to a police decoy Howe had voted to deny food to hungry people beyond the borders of the United States, it is probable that he would still be a member of Congress. Any member of Congress can elicit cheers from an audience—in Utah or Illinois or any other state—by denouncing foreign economic aid with great sounds of piety: "We should stop pouring money down the drain in these foreign countries and take care of our own people. If it's a choice of foreign aid or reducing taxes, I'm for reducing taxes." Those of us in politics like applause, and those few words, delivered with a little bombast, will produce an audience reaction that will warm the heart of any speaker—except one who thinks.

Just to use the one gauge of a vote on foreign aid (and one gauge should rarely be used to measure a public official), Howe voted for the two-year authorization for international development assistance (aid for the poor overseas) during his one term in Congress, and in 1977 his successor voted against a similar bill.

Which is the greater evil, soliciting a police decoy or voting against food for hungry people? Who committed the greater immorality, Allen Howe or the people of his district?

The personal morality/public morality issue hit the nation's front pages in mid-1983 with the disclosure that two members of the House had sexual relations with pages. In the case of Representative Dan Crane, a Republican from Illinois, it involved a seventeen-year-old girl; and in the case of Representative Gerry Studds, a Democrat from Massachusetts, it involved a seventeen-year-old boy. The House Ethics Committee recommended a reprimand of both. Representative Newton Gingrich suggested to the press, but did not propose, expulsion. The House chose the middle ground of the rarely used official censure.

To the credit of the House, the debate on the matter did not take on a holier-than-thou air, though there was an almost universal assumption that both members had been guilty of a serious breach of ethics by taking advantage of pages.

But the House is not alone in having to face up to a difficult decision. Citizens in each of their districts must do the same. Studds won election in 1982 with a 68.7 percent majority, and Crane by a much narrower 52.1 percent. Initial press reports show greater post-disclosure public support for the incumbent in Studds's district than in Crane's. That—plus the winning margins in 1982—indicates a Studds victory but not a Crane victory. But history suggests that the contriteness of Crane may wear better than the defense of his actions by Studds. Complicating things further is Studds's acknowledged homosexuality.

It is easy for citizens in those two districts to make judgments on this issue and this issue alone. It will be a consideration. But where they and their opponents stand on questions relating to the arms race, the nation's economy, and help to the desperate within our own country and in other nations should also be

considerations. Because what they did is much easier to understand than, for example, a position on the MX missile—both for
reporters and the citizenry—their personal defects will be on
public display, their policy strengths and weaknesses will be much
less understood.

Citizens cannot ignore the question of conduct, but closely
equating personal morality and public morality may result in bad
public policy. There is a tendency, as columnist George Will has
observed, for the public to "dive into the shallow end of every
pool."[11] Great attention to personal conduct and little study of
the great issues is precisely that. Solon, the great Athenian leader
who brought about peaceful revolution, would not have been
selected the leader of Athens had the standards of personal morality been too high. An old poem contains some truth:

> King Solomon and King David
> Led very merry lives,
> With their very many concubines
> And very many wives
> Until old age o'ertook them
> With its very many qualms
> Then King Solomon wrote the Proverbs
> And King David wrote the Psalms.[12]

David was, on balance, a good ruler who had major personal
flaws; Solomon, a less sensitive ruler, has a generally good image,
despite his personal and public mistakes. Human beings have
flaws. Those who rule for us should provide example as well as
seek justice. But if the public expects too much by way of example, inevitably there will be great disappointments.

The struggle to do what is right and just and good is not easy,
neither for the conscientious public official nor for the conscientious citizens who select their leaders.

☆ 3 ☆

Two and Two Sometimes
Equal Five

Things are seldom what they seem;
Skim milk masquerades as cream.
> — *H.M.S. Pinafore*[1]

The process of translating a high moral principle into sub-
stantive, enforceable language has been a complex one, and
that is why the agreement reflected in this compromise
amendment is so important.
> —Senator H. John Heinz III,
> *Congressional Record*, May 5, 1977[2]

Morality, thou deadly bane,
Thy tens o' thousands thou hast slain!
> —Robert Burns, 1786[3]

I t was a simple request. In 1977, my daughter, then sixteen
years old, asked me to grow a beard. There is nothing immoral about that. But if I had started appearing on television in
my conservative southern Illinois district with a beard, and cam-
paigned throughout the district well whiskered, I would have
lost votes—maybe not enough to lose the next election, but who
knows? If I had heeded her request (and usually I find myself
doing that) and had been narrowly defeated by a candidate who
could provide no leadership, who would oppose aid to the hungry and help to education, what might have appeared to be a
perfectly proper action would have been a foolish and unjustified
risk.

That's an oversimplified illustration of how moral actions can cause immoral results. Some of the most bitter wars have been carried on in the name of religion, which many regard as the basis of morality. Through the centuries Jews have been persecuted by Christians who believed their own actions were moral. History is filled with gross examples of good causes gone askew.

Public Law 480 is more commonly known as "Food for Peace." Under this program food is given to areas of great need, or sales are made in some form of concession to a country that has severe shortages. It is one of the better U.S. programs, though warped in part because tobacco is one of the agricultural products that can go to a recipient country under P.L. 480. There are commercial advantages to the recipient nation having tobacco, and there are domestic advantages to the United States, a producing nation selling it. But only the naive do not know that tobacco (at least in the form of cigarette smoking) causes serious health problems. For the United States to send tobacco to a poor country under the label "Food for Peace" strikes some as ridiculous.

When the P.L. 480 program came up for renewal in 1977, Representative James Johnson, Republican of Colorado (since retired), offered an amendment to prohibit the use of the Food for Peace program to send tobacco to poor countries. He told his House colleagues:

> In 1978, it is estimated we are going to provide $24 million worth of tobacco products to five different countries. This would provide food assistance for 890,000 people. . . . It would be perhaps appropriate to give it away to our enemies, instead . . . of our friends. It seems to me a terrible inconsistency to spend all the money we do every year on education about the dangers of tobacco, to spend all the money we do on cancer research and to warn the American public as we have, at the same time to finance through this program $24 million of [tobacco] aid that would feed 890,000 people.[4]

What could be a clearer moral issue?

As the debate took place, three or four of us huddled in the back of the House trying to determine how we should vote. We were not discussing the merits of the Johnson amendment. The question we had to determine was: If the Johnson amendment carried, would the seventy-one members of the House in whose districts tobacco is a significant crop, plus twenty-eight with larger amounts—more than fifty thousand acres of tobacco—vote for the final passage of the bill? Before the discussion could reach any clear conclusion, the amendment came up for a vote. With some apprehension, I voted for the Johnson amendment. The amendment passed, and so did the bill. It's a story with a happy ending, at least temporarily.

Of the twenty-eight members with substantial tobacco crops in their district, only two—Representatives Jack Brinkley of Georgia and Charles Bennett of Florida—voted for the Johnson amendment. Of these same twenty-eight members, only two voted for the final passage of the bill after the Johnson amendment had been accepted: Brinkley and Representative Richard Preyer of North Carolina. The vote was 61–10 against the Johnson amendment for members whose districts include less substantial amounts of tobacco. On final passage, the same two groups voted 26–2 against passage and 58–13 against passage. As it turned out, the bill passed by a comfortable margin (252–158). If the vote had been closer, the adoption of the Johnson amendment would have killed the bill. Then my "moral" vote would have denied food to millions of hungry people, clearly an immoral result.[5]

The conscientious member has to struggle with that kind of a vote. Years after his House service, Jerry Voorhis recalled: "I remember as if it were yesterday the terrible distress of spirit I would feel after casting some of these votes on highly controversial measures. For several days the only arguments I could think of would be the ones on the opposite side from the way I had voted."[6]

President Jimmy Carter's emphasis on human rights, President Reagan's deemphasis of human rights, and some congressional battles in this area also illustrate that purity of purpose and consequences are not necessarily wedded.

"The ideals of this nation" is a phrase many of us utter with ease and assurance. Unfortunately, too often those ideals have been clouded by our actions when in international politics we have been "realistic" and "pragmatic." Just as taking moral stands without consideration of the ends can be counterproductive, so in the same way a compromise of beliefs to secure what appear to be morally justifiable ends can be deceptive and self-defeating. "Bad means corrupt good ends," Mahatma Gandhi used to say. If our aim is peace and stability and self-determination for the people of South Vietnam, and if "enemy" soldiers are using Cambodia to come into Vietnam, then it is asserted we are justified in bombing and invading Cambodia. Unfortunately, not enough people questioned the validity of that assumption, and the result was neither significant help for South Vietnam nor assistance to the people of Cambodia. Cambodia ended up with one of the most repressive regimes in history. There are many students of that period who believe our action, though well motivated, caused the crumbling of a much less repressive government in Cambodia (now Kampuchea).

In part, the Cambodian action resulted from a mistaken notion that beyond our borders our actions can fall far short of the nation's ideals, and that we can effectively serve those ideals through the end result. There has been a largely unspoken assumption that within the United States we must stand for freedom, but that foreign policy can be dictated solely by what serves the economic and defense interests of the nation. "We have to keep our feet on the ground," a Reagan administration official told me as I requested further pressure for human rights in an Asian country. I understand that, but I could not help but recall what my former House colleague William Hungate, now a federal judge, used to say: "Show me a man with both feet on the ground and I'll show you a man who can't change his pants."

From World War II to the Carter years, the two presidencies that moved the greatest distance from the "pragmatic" philosophy in foreign affairs, where our oratory and actions came close to being blended, were those of Harry S Truman and John F. Kennedy. We had the Marshall Plan and the Point Four program under Truman and the Peace Corps and the Alliance for Progress under Kennedy. When the Kennedy era ended, the United States slipped badly. Vietnam devastated the Lyndon Johnson presidency, though foreign affairs had not been his strength or interest even during his Senate years. Richard Nixon and Gerald Ford contributed to an improved East-West climate, but their administrations made no great attempt either to appeal to or understand the less developed nations.

Many of us cheered the willingness of the Carter administration to speak forthrightly about human rights, to identify with the hopes of the repressed in Africa (which it did much better than any previous administration), to urge greater cultural sensitivity to the languages and customs of other nations. We stand for freedom and justice as a nation, and the president should remind us here at home of our ideals as well as proclaim them beyond our borders.

But caution is needed. Others sometimes see our shortcomings and inconsistencies more clearly than we ourselves do. In the process of letting others know our beliefs, we should not alienate by appearing sanctimonious. I appreciated President Carter's willingness to admit our shortcomings. If we speak of human rights with an air of pompous superiority (as sometimes we do), we shall have few listeners, and even fewer who are sympathetic. Our deeds speak more loudly than our words, and if we can promote the concepts of freedom and self-determination without being too vocal, both our nation and other nations will be better served.

Until the invasion of Grenada—not likely to be viewed by history as one of our finer moments—there appeared to be a gradual and much-needed improvement in President Reagan's performance in foreign policy, an improvement that followed a start that was both disappointing and breathtaking. The new commander of the ship of state conducted himself in such a way that he made clear to the world his lack of knowledge in foreign affairs, unfortunately an affliction that has plagued too many of our presidents.

Helping improve the Reagan performance has been the appointment of George Schultz as secretary of state. But unlike the Carter presidency, which made clear the priority of human rights, the new Reagan administration gave—and too often still gives—every signal to the world's dictators that human rights is a bit of icing on the cake, we are really only concerned with their position in the East-West struggle. The government of Argentina felt it had a new, cozier relationship with the United States. Not only did our retreat on human rights dim the fires of hope that had been kindled in homes all over the globe, but we also failed as an agent of restraint in the invasion of the Falklands.

The Union of South Africa feels much more comfortable with the Reagan administration's nominal opposition to the repressive apartheid policies than with the Carter administration's more aggressive stance. But whom are we fooling with our acquiescence to South Africa's self-destructive policies? South Africa is headed down the road to unbelievable violence unless the United States and other nations can force that nation to reappraise its policies. By our audible silence we alienate much of Africa; we fail to speak out for the oppressed who need our support; and we stand mute while the nation with the strongest economy in all of Africa moves closer and closer to a time bomb that will blow it apart. Can anyone believe such a policy on our part is either moral or sensible?

Caution, however, must be exercised before we make judgments on how we should promote our beliefs. For example, if our public posture on the human rights issue so clouds relations with the Soviets that armament agreements are not possible, and at the same time does no good for the oppressed within the Soviet Union, then our moral stance brings about an immoral result. We have to determine more effective ways of achieving our goals.

Jewish emigration from the Soviet Union receives strong support in the United States for sound reasons: the undisguised anti-Semitism and general repression of freedom in the USSR, and the massacre of the Jews by Hitler. This is more than an academic issue with me. I have visited with many Soviet Jews, including the wife and mother of Anatoly Scharansky and the wife of Dr. Sakharov, as well as others who are part of the small, gallant band of Soviet dissidents who dare to stand up. In 1983, on my last visit to the Soviet Union, I was in the Moscow apartment of Professor and Mrs. Naum Meiman, a Jewish couple who want to emigrate to Israel. The seventy-one-year-old professor has spoken out on behalf of freedom and implementation of the Helsinki Accord signed by the Soviet Union. There is nothing the Sovet Union could do that would generate more goodwill for themselves than to let people like Anatoly Scharansky and the Meimans emigrate.

Jewish emigration, primarily to Israel, reached its peak in 1973. At that time the Soviets were increasing trade with the United States, and we were discussing granting them "most favored nation" trade status, which gives economic encouragement for trade with the United States. A factor that played a role in what subsequently developed involved Secretary of State Henry Kissinger's "style." Most members of Congress respected his ability and approved the majority of his thrusts in foreign policy, but we generally had the feeling that he was less than candid. On this score briefings given by Kissinger and those by then Secretary of Defense James Schlesinger tended to differ. We came away from the Kissinger briefings a little puzzled about what had happened and what might happen, but certain that Kissinger had not been completely open. On the other hand, many of us disagreed with Schlesinger's conclusions, but we left his briefings feeling that he had been honest with us.

In that climate the late Senator Henry Jackson of Washington and Representative Charles Vanik of Ohio acted. Jackson and Vanik introduced an amendment that said the Soviets could have most-favored-nation trade status only if they agreed to let Jews emigrate from the Soviet Union. Both shared a suspicion with most members of Congress that Nixon and Kissinger were not pushing the issue aggressively. The Jackson-Vanik amendment turned out to be well intentioned but fruitless. A bludgeon when a scalpel might have worked, it probably contributed to a negative Soviet reaction and a slowing of emigration. The heavy-handed rigidity of a congressional amendment turned out to be an inadequate substitute for the more flexible and less visible approach the executive branch might have provided.

In retrospect, the Jackson-Vanik amendment was a mistake, a calculated risk that might have worked, a risk taken when the executive branch appeared indifferent. No nation wants to knuckle under publicly to another nation. A morally right cause suffered because Congress voted for what is morally right. Two and two sometimes equal five.* If Soviet–U.S. relations improve

---

*Although I believe, in hindsight, that enactment of the original Jackson-Vanik amendment was a mistake, I do not favor repeal of it unless there is movement by the Soviets. Repeal would accomplish nothing, other than the appearance of a Soviet victory. If there is movement on the emigration question by the Soviets, I would vote for repeal of Jackson-Vanik.

markedly, there will be an improvement in the emigration picture. But a better U.S.–USSR climate is the only thing that can bring it about.

In 1906 the U.S. ambassador to Saint Petersburg asked Secretary of State Elihu Root whether there should be a protest regarding persecution of the Jews in Russia. Root replied:

> I think it may do some good, although I do not feel sure of it. . . . I am sure that to publish . . . the fact that such a dispatch has been sent would do harm, and serious harm to the unfortunate people whom we desire to help. Any possible good effect must be looked for in absolutely confidential communication to the Russian government.[7]

Frequently confidential action is much more effective, but unfortunately the record of history is that too often confidential action has become a cover-up for no action. The United States, like most nations, frequently has found it easier to ignore persecution than to protest it.

Representative Thomas Harkin of Iowa headed another attempt to push, via an amendment, the cause of human rights. Harkin was serving as an administrative aide to Representative Neal Smith of Iowa when he discovered the "tiger cages" in South Vietnam used for political prisoners. During the Gerald Ford presidency Harkin introduced an amendment that mandated the United States to vote against loans in two of the international lending agencies to countries that have "a consistent pattern of gross violations of internationally recognized human rights." An exception could be made where "such assistance will directly benefit the needy people in such country." The two lending agencies affected were the Inter-American Development Bank and the African Development Fund.

The Ford administration worked against the amendment, arguing that it deprived the executive branch of flexibility. Representative Millicent Fenwick of New Jersey said that to deprive people of any country of the chance to lift themselves out of economic misery because we disapprove of their government is neither rational nor humane. No one argued against applying some pressure to repressive regimes to grant their people more freedom; the question was simply how to do it. Despite the Fenwick appeals and similar arguments by Representatives Jonathan Bingham of New York and Donald Fraser of Minnesota (now mayor of Minneapolis), the Harkin amendment carried.

The same issue emerged early in the Carter administration. Representative Herman Badillo of New York, a member of the Banking and Currency Committee, joined Harkin in sponsoring the same amendment, applying it to the other international lending agencies. The agencies stated that since their mandate required them to pay no attention to internal politics, they could not accept funds with such restrictions, and without U.S. money other nations would not likely contribute funds. That, some argued, could have meant the end of these vital international agencies—a result a few looked upon with favor, but not Harkin and Badillo. When the issue emerged in the Banking and Currency Committee, the chairman of that committee, Representative Henry Reuss of Wisconsin, offered a substitute calling for the United States to "advance the cause of human rights . . . by seeking to channel assistance toward countries other than those whose governments engage in a consistent pattern of gross violation of internationally recognized human rights."[8]

At first the Carter administration resisted the Reuss substitute, but it soon realized that the Reuss proposal was its only chance of defeating the less flexible Harkin amendment. *Flexible* became a key word on both sides. To the administration it meant an ability to move ahead on human rights and other areas without the stumbling block of a rigid Harkin amendment. To many members *flexibility* sounded like the same word the Nixon-Kissinger forces had used—as an excuse for doing far too little.

Senator Daniel P. Moynihan of New York, whose ambassadorial and U.N. background gave him insights, noted: "It is entirely correct to say (as was repeatedly said during all those 'years of silence' in Washington) that quiet diplomacy is a much more effective way to obtain near-term concessions from totalitarian regimes with respect to particular individuals who seek our help. But the large result of proceeding in this fashion is that the democracies accommodate to the dictators."[9]

Representative Don Fraser of Minnesota, long a champion of civil liberties, felt that the new administration should not be judged by the Nixon standard, that Carter was acting positively. Harkin countered that he wanted the language in the law for future presidents also.

The *Chicago Tribune* editorialized:

> Foreign aid . . . is too delicate and complex a matter to be governed by a single, rigid formula, however nobly inspired, that ignores both economic and world politics. The advantage of indirect aid through presumably hard-nosed international agencies is that it is—or at least is more likely to be—based on solid economic judgments with respect to such questions as whether it helps to make a country more self-supporting and whether it is likely, in the long run, to contribute to the sort of world where freedom and human rights prevail.[10]

The morning before the decision in the House, Harkin and Reuss met in my office, along with Assistant Secretary of the Treasury Fred Bergsten, to try to fashion some middle ground. Nothing firm emerged from our meeting, except a possible compromise that Reuss and Bergsten agreed to: keep the Harkin language on the two international lending agencies where it already exists, and apply the Reuss language to the others. Harkin, meeting with us despite a fever, later rejected the proposal.* One of the arguments made during this attempt at a compromise was that if Indonesia, where there reportedly were between twenty-five and forty thousand political prisoners, would agree to release ten thousand prisoners in exchange for support on a loan, the Reuss amendment would give the United States the chance to move ahead; the Harkin amendment would not.

Carter himself made an appeal to a group of us meeting at a breakfast at the White House on another matter. Without referring to the Harkin amendment by name, he asked that we give him "a chance to get some things done in the area of human rights. If a year from now we're not doing what we should be doing, then put an amendment like that on." Despite Carter's

---

*We'll never know how many times history has been shaped by chance events such as someone having a fever. Whether it would have made a difference in this case, I don't know. But Harkin understandably was not in a mood to sit around a table and discuss complex international issues. A fever, a fight with your spouse, a headache, a stubbed toe—these types of things change history in ways we generally will never know.

appeal, the Harkin amendment carried over the Reuss alternative in the House.

In the Senate, James Abourzek of South Dakota sponsored the Harkin amendment. The same coalition formed in the Senate, with Senator Hubert Humphrey heading the opposition. Humphrey, joined by Senators Alan Cranston of California and Edward Kennedy of Massachusetts, defeated the Harkin proposal 50–43. The conference committee language, closer to the Reuss proposal, carried despite the opposition of Harkin and Badillo, who had written to their House colleagues about the conference language: "We are shocked that so soon after living through what has become known as the Imperial Presidency there are members of this body who are willing to include in legislation language which allows the executive branch to unilaterally negate [human rights mandates]."[11]

But the fundamental question is not easily answered: How do you most effectively move ahead in the field of human rights internationally? Congressional action gives the executive the chance to say to foreign leaders, "I'd like to help you, but I have to work with Congress, and they're very sticky on human rights." The ideal answer is for Congress to establish broad policy and let the administration carry it out with maximum flexibility. But when an administration has no great concern for the issue of human rights, should a more clumsy legislative tool be used? We should not, for example, in the name of human rights, cut off our contacts with any government, for that does not help the people of that country, nor does it serve the best interests of American foreign policy.

The massive bloodshed and pain caused by the Vietnam War could have been over sooner had Congress acted quickly. It finally ended, not because of executive action, but because Congress cut off funds. Stung by Vietnam and apparent executive indifference to the tragic dimensions of that struggle, Congress acted with a heavy hand.

Congress has to pick its way carefully, aware that sometimes what appear to be right answers are wrong answers, and what appear to be wrong answers are right answers.

The Chinese have a saying: "Embarrassment leads to anger." How do we promote human rights without angering other nations, threatening world stability? How do we handle the human rights issue so that it does not become simply an empty slogan spouted by one of the major powers? How do we in Congress get a Reagan administration to pay more attention to human rights abuses in the non-Communist countries? Is there a danger that the people of our nation—and others—are looking for quick results on human rights when progress usually can be measured only in the most limited terms, two years from now or ten years from now? Will the public tire and lose interest? To talk about human rights to people who are desperately hungry is like talking Arabic in Guatemala; few will understand. And the most basic human right is the right to eat. How do we tie these together?

"Because we are free we can never be indifferent to the fate of freedom elsewhere," Jimmy Carter told the nation in his inaugural address. I joined in the applause when I heard those words. But we must be practical and patient as we apply them. If we expect too much, if we fail to recognize that progress will be slow and vary from country to country, if we are too removed from reality in our approach, if we fail to remember that our own record is not unblemished, the result will be harm rather than good. We must also examine our motives. For example, it usually makes more political sense domestically to denounce the Soviet Union on human rights—knowing it will do little good— than it is to meet privately with them to discuss our human rights concerns, which sometimes does do some good.

In his 1945 State of the Union message, Franklin D. Roosevelt said: "Perfectionism, no less than isolationism or imperialism or power politics, may obstruct the paths to international peace. Let us not forget that the retreat to isolationism a quarter of a century ago was started not by a direct attack against international cooperation but against the alleged imperfections of the peace."[12]

He was correct, but so was the poet Archibald MacLeish when he wrote: "There are those . . . who will say that the liberation of humanity, the freedom of man and mind, is nothing but a dream. They are right. It is. It is the American dream."[13]

☆ 4 ☆

Money

[Governor] Henry Horner [of Illinois] was the real goods. . . . He collaborated with men who were purchaseable without becoming purchaseable himself. He got to high places without selling his soul.

—Carl Sandburg[1]

The acquisition of campaign funds has become an obsession on the part of nearly every candidate for federal office. The obsession leads the candidates to solicit and accept money from those most able to provide it, and to adjust their behavior in office to the need for money—and the fear that a challenger might be able to obtain more. . . . Until the problem of money is dealt with, it is unrealistic to expect the political process to improve in any other respect.

—Elizabeth Drew[2]

When a fellow says, "It ain't the money but the principle of the thing," it's the money.

—Frank McKinney Hubbard[3]

Discuss politics with any two members of the House or Senate and within a few minutes the conversation will turn to money. Evan Davis, a respected reporter for the *Southern Illinoisan*, asked me, "Are you going to do anything during these first six months in Congress other than talk about the budget and money?"

The preoccupation of members with money is dictated in part by the unprecedented deficits the federal government now faces.

But we also set the national priorities as we determine where we appropriate the money. Congress can approve the most high-sounding programs, but if those programs are not funded the carefully drafted phrases of the law are meaningless. Determining spending priorities is no easy task for a well-informed Congress, even if one assumes only the noblest of intentions and that Congress will totally ignore pressure from special interest groups.

But the decisions of government are not made in such a pristine atmosphere. Money not only determines the priorities of the federal government, it also determines who sits in Congress and makes those priorities. Money too often warps the decisions of even the most nobly motivated.

The public perceives that lobbyists hand out large chunks of crisp, green bills in exchange for passage or defeat of legislation. Sometimes that does happen. The videotaped escapades of seven members of the House and Senate who took FBI money, thinking it came from an Arab sheik, confirm that perception. The word *bribe* is originally a French word, meaning a scrap of bread or money given to a beggar. There are still some political beggars around taking bribes. But my impression is that there are few in Congress who follow that path. It is less of a problem today than a century ago, or probably at any time in the nation's history. During George Washington's first year as president, a bonding proposal put forward in good faith by Alexander Hamilton turned into a tidy profit for almost forty members of the House and Senate, including Hamilton's father-in-law, Philip Schuyler.

During Earl Long's tenure as one of Louisiana's most colorful politicians, he described one fellow Louisiana politician as follows: "Jimmie Davis loves money like a hog loves slop."[4] In 1930 H. L. Mencken wrote: "The typical lawmaker of today is a man wholly devoid of principle—a mere counter in a grotesque and knavish game. If the right pressure could be applied to him he would be cheerfully in favor of polygamy, astrology, or cannibalism."[5] Today the major money problem that plagues legislators and that should concern the public is campaign financing. "CONGRESS FOR SALE" screams the cover of the *New Republic*.[6] It almost sounds like a return to early eighteenth century England when seats in Parliament were openly advertised for sale in the London *Times*. "The best Congress money can buy" is the overworked line in at least a dozen articles. Our present system of financing congressional campaigns, as well as gubernatorial and other races, is a national embarrassment.

Because I won by less than 1 percent in 1980, early in the 1982 campaign I was targeted for defeat by several groups, including the National Conservative Political Action Committee (NCPAC) and the Republican National Committee (RNC). (Later in the campaign the RNC dropped me as a target.) As a consequence, in 1982 I spent far more than I have spent in any previous election year: $413,477. But that is less than the $746,092 and $648,925 spent by the two candidates in the congressional district north of mine, and less than the $2.5 million spent in one House race in Massachusetts, and the $2 million spent in one House race in Tennessee. Five candidates for the House spent more than $1 million. Most targeted incumbents spent more than I did. "Politics has got so expensive it takes a lot of money even to get beat," Will Rogers once said.[7] His observation is even more appropriate today.

The system of financing campaigns is bad, not in the way most news articles suggest, but in a more subtle though equally harmful way. There may be some members of Congress who vote for or against a bill specifically because of a campaign contribution, but the much commoner problem is that campaign contributors have greater access to policy makers, and access spells votes. It is natural for a candidate to feel a sense of gratitude toward those who contribute to a campaign. You listen carefully to people toward whom you feel a sense of gratitude. The inequity is that those with limited income do not have such access. There is also the subtle, unspoken understanding between legislator and donor. When Jane Green comes to me with her views on legislation, or a request, she does not need to tell me that she has given me a thousand-dollar campaign contribution. She knows it, and she is reasonably sure I know it. Only rarely is anyone crude enough to remind me before presenting his or her views. The subtle pressures are there, however.

I schedule open office hours around my district in southern Illinois, in part to make sure than anyone who wants to see me can do so. But that approach is hardly an answer to a national problem. The political system should not be structured to grant the powerful much readier access to policy makers than that available to those with limited resources and those in great need.

Certainly I cannot be expected to take every phone call that comes into my office myself. If Mrs. Jones or Mr. Smith has a food stamp problem and wants to talk to me personally, sometimes I can take the call, but generally I cannot. Someone on my staff will handle the matter. With 520,000 people in my district there are practical limitations on my time. But if Jane Green calls, and she has made a thousand-dollar campaign contribution, I usually make myself available. I hardly suggest that this is right; but it is the reality of the situation, in my office and in every other congressional office. It means that people who have money have greater ability to influence a House or Senate member than those without money. I listen to donors. I frequently have to tell them that I disagree; but many issues are what we call "close calls," where it would be easy to vote either way, where there is enough good and bad on both sides that you have to weigh carefully how you vote. I have never consciously said to myself, "He or she or this group gave me a big campaign contribution. I think I'll vote with them." Sometimes I bend over backward to examine my motives for voting a certain way. Nevertheless, there have been instances in which I have heard more of one side of an issue than another, where a toss of the coin (an apt phrase in this context) could determine my vote because the arguments seemed so equal and I leaned in the direction of those who were my supporters. All politicians admire and respect the good judgment of those who contribute to their campaigns! One of the nation's largest contributors has said that dialogue with politicians "is a fine thing, but with a little money they hear you better."[8] It is difficult to argue with the conclusion reached by former Representative Millicent Fenwick: "Why is this happening in our electoral process? The terrible truth, I believe, is that these gifts pay off."[9] This is why the least fortunate in our society too often get shortchanged. This has been particularly true during the Reagan years.

One common misconception is that the government wastes huge amounts of money on the poor. When I speak to groups about federal deficits, I almost invariably get suggestions about cutting back on welfare. Our welfare system does need an over-haul, a shift to encourage people to be participating members of our society by providing training and jobs. Fifty years ago the nation made a sound decision that it would not let people starve, and now we must face a decision on whether we will pay people for doing nothing or pay people for doing something. We have backed into the preference of paying people for doing nothing, an unhappy answer for these people and for the nation. But if you take the traditional welfare progams—food stamps, Aid to Families with Dependent Children, and the Supplemental Security Income Program—the total for Fiscal Year 1983 is $32 billion, only 4 percent of the total budget. Most government expenditures assist middle- and upper-income Americans more than others: highways, universities, housing (interest deductions on mortgages), airports, and so on. Today, not many would agree with the eighteenth-century English observer who said: "Every-one but an idiot knows that the lower classes must be kept poor or they will never be industrious."[10] That hostility has changed to indifference, or to the belief—held by many in power now—that if you help those at the top of the economic ladder, those at the bottom will automatically benefit. Comedian Dick Gregory has a point when he says: "Think about all the cocktails that will be sipped this year and written off as business expenses on in-come tax forms. Yet a poor mother has to go through all sorts of trouble to get a free meal for her baby."[11]

Though the poor continue to be the least potent group polit-ically, the sensitivity of government to the less fortunate has improved over the centuries, but there remains some truth to Sir Thomas More's observation in the sixteenth century: "When I consider . . . all these commonwealths which nowadays every-where do flourish, so God help me, I can perceive nothing but a certain conspiracy of rich men, procuring their own commod-ities under the name and title of the commonwealth."[12] To the extent that our government, or any government, does that, it plays into the hands of the Marxists. Marxism's appeal is not what it proposes, but what it opposes. During the first Reagan years there was a huge increase in military expenditures (which arguably could be said to benefit all elements of society), record-breaking tax cuts with benefits overwhelmingly skewed to those of upper income, and substantial cuts in programs that help the poor.

How could a humanitarian country like ours, which has performed such unprecedentedly generous acts as the Marshall Plan, helping the world's poor after World War II, do this? The answer is three-pronged. First, those whose eyes start to glisten when they talk about helping the poor by assisting those in high-income brackets have at least temporarily dominated the administration's decision making. Second, there are those in Congress who genuinely have the same philosophical approach. Third, far too many in Congress listen to the big contributors rather than the big sufferers. Although the Republican party is particularly susceptible to this temptation, too many of my own party are equally vulnerable.

Campaign contributions have other effects, too. The present system robs the candidate and public official of time. We already do far too much talking and too little listening, reading, and reflecting. I have to worry about my own fund raising and spend time on it, and I have to worry about fund raising opportunities I may be creating for my opponent.

One of the finest public servants I have known, Senator Paul Douglas of Illinois, wrote: "Tests do not always come in open conflicts between what is right or wrong, but over shadings, where it is hard to find guiding principles. They can emerge when one is tired and off guard, or in the soft requests of a friend. But the wrong road can lead you farther and farther from the true path, and to ultimate ruin."[13]

I am grateful to many people who contribute to me despite my votes. My longtime friend and an outstanding citizen, George Bader, who died a few years ago, probably gave me ten thousand dollars over the years for various campaigns. He called me one day and said, "Paul, I've never asked you for a favor or a vote in all these years, have I?"

"No, George, you have not."

"This farm bill that's coming up tomorrow is really important to me. I hope you'll vote for it."

"George, I hate to tell you, but that's a bad bill." I explained my reasons without any interruption at the other end of the phone. And then:

"Well, you son of a bitch."

That ended the conversation. The next day he called and told me that though he disagreed with me, he respected me more than ever for not going along. He was an even stronger supporter after that. But there are not many people as fine as George Bader. If the merits of the bill had been close, I probably would have voted with my friend and contributor.

Since the candidate who spends the most money generally wins, there are far too many candidates shaping their views to meet the financial needs of a campaign, rather than the actual needs of the country. The combination of polling and campaign contributions has resulted in far too many members worshiping at the shrines of public opinion and campaign money; in the process they get elected, but their ability or inclination to provide real leadership is meager. The candidate wins but the nation loses.

Because of the election threat I faced in 1982, for the first time I hired a professional to do my television work. The production costs alone came to seventy-five thousand dollars. I am embarrassed by that figure, but I would be more embarrassed had I lost. I also hired a professional to raise money by mail. (Democrats have a national direct mail list of approximately 200,000 contributors; Republicans, who have been at it much longer, have one of 1,700,000.) The television producer packaged my views as attractively as possible, and that did not bother me; I try to do the same in my speeches. But in direct mail, the more extreme your position, the more effective the appeal for funds. One of the most successful mail solicitors comments: "The shriller you are, the better it is to raise money."[14] The initial draft of each letter my experts wrote screamed at the readers, virtually assuring them that if they did not contribute to my campaign it would be the end of civilization. I toned the letters down, though they retained a touch of that quality. To be effective, mail solicitation, an increasingly significant aspect of fund raising, has to both tear at the heart and promise to save the Union. The money-by-mail experts assure me that appeals for money with the emphasis placed on what a responsible member of the House or Senate you will be and spelling out some of your views simply do not bring results. Unfortunately, this often means the election of people with extreme views, or people who are trapped by the extreme views expressed in their own letters.

The public already has a generally low opinion of members of Congress, but the cynicism that our present campaign funding system generates—and should generate—breeds greater hostility to our form of government. One of the questions pollster Louis Harris asks regularly is whether people agree with the statement: "The people running the country don't really care what happens to you." The affirmative response to that was 26 percent in 1976 and 50 percent in 1982. Sixty-three percent "of young people between the ages of eighteen and twenty-nine feel alienated . . . twelve points higher than in 1978."[15] Seventy-four percent of blacks and 65 percent of Hispanics feel alienated. The response to a similar question asked by the University of Michigan's Center for Political Studies reflects the same trend. Decades ago journalist Oscar Ameringer noted: "Politics is the gentle art of getting votes from the poor and campaign funds from the rich, by promising to protect each from the other."[16] That cynical description is as appropriate today as it was then, and the public mood reflects that fact.

Never before has the White House been used so effectively to raise funds as was the Reagan White House in 1982. And yet the following quotation, attributed to Lee Atwater, deputy assistant to the president for political affairs, remained buried in a magazine article rather than exploding into a major news story: "The story of this off-year [1982] election is that we've marshalled our resources and bought one or two Senate seats and fifteen to twenty House seats, and that's really good."[17] The *Wall Street Journal* quotes Rich Bond of the Republican National Committee as lining up two votes for the 1982 budget cuts by saying to members, "Look, what if I can guarantee we'll max out [give you the maximum allowed under the law] on you? We'll help you do a quick-and-dirty newsletter, make a commercial, organize a town meeting."[18] Why shouldn't the public be cynical? Unfortunately, cynicism doesn't help. There is a veneer of sophistication to cynicism, but the nation needs to change the system, and those too deeply mired in the quicksands of cynicism will do nothing to improve it.

The use of money in campaigns is not a new phenomenon. When George Washington ran for the Virginia House of Burgesses in 1757 he found that military responsibilities kept him from the campaign trail. He arranged for his supporters to distribute the following: twenty-eight gallons of rum, fifty gallons of rum punch, thirty-four gallons of wine, forty-six gallons of beer, and two gallons of cider royal. Washington wrote to his campaign manager: "I hope . . . all had enough."[19] Since there were 391 voters, that averaged a quart and a half per man, a substantial expenditure even by today's standards. However inappropriate Washington's actions may have been, they were wholesome compared to the present system of soliciting contributions from those who seek legislative favors, and then dispensing money in a much more calculated way.

Sometimes money can backfire. A measure was introduced to use the legislative veto power of the Congress over the Federal Trade Commission (FTC) regulations to negate a provision the FTC had called for requiring dealers to certify the known defects of a used car before it is sold. I have serious questions about the wisdom of legislative vetoes in the first place—the Supreme Court has since ruled them unconstitutional—and my initial inclination was to support the new regulation. Then Robert O'Brien, a friend in the automobile business with a good public conscience, contacted me and said the regulation would result in more harm to the public than good. During the debate, Representative John Seiberling of Ohio said that although he had received no campaign funds from the automobile dealers (funding had become part of the debate), he had examined the FTC proposal and said it would end up as a paradise for lawyers but do the public no good. I asked Representative William Lehman of Florida, who had once been in the automobile business, what he thought. He said that if the FTC regulation were approved it would result in responsible dealers getting out of the used car business, that only the "fly by nights" would remain. I voted with the automobile dealers. Newspaper stories stressed the role of campaign contributions from car dealers. A friend whose vote on the issue surprised me told me in response to my inquiry, "I had to vote against the automobile dealers. The newspapers were making a big thing out of the contributions." He had received a large contribution. I had received none. The automobile dealers were victorious, but the issue was not decided strictly on its merits. Would they have won anyway? Did they lose votes because of their contributions and the attendant publicity? No one knows the answers.

Representative Berkley Bedell of Iowa commented: "The greatest evil is the knowledge you carry with you that campaign contributions are part of the voting and part of your future. You can't escape being aware of that reality as you vote."[20]

Another problem is the obvious imbalance between expenditures of different candidates and the expenditures of different political parties. In the 1980 national campaign the Republicans were able to spend $64.6 million in "hard money" (money that can be contributed to federal candidates directly within legal limitations), compared to $13.9 million by the Democrats. When you add the "soft money" (everything from union dues to corporate money that can go to state and local candidates or for causes such as voter registration), and the expenditures of "independent committees" unregulated by the limitations faced by candidates, the total expenditure by the Republicans in Texas alone roughly equaled the total spent nationally by the Democrats. For the 1981–82 election cycle, Republican party committees outraised the Democratic party committees $153 million to $27 million. At the end of 1982, the Republican committees emerged with a surplus of $6.3 million and the Democrats with a deficit of $2.2 million. Just as disconcerting, in 1981–82 the Democrats increased their fund raising by 45 percent, and the Republican increase was six times the Democratic dollar amount. The situation is bad, and it is getting worse. Both parties and the nation are losers.

A further complication is that under a Supreme Court ruling, expenditures by "independent committees" are unlimited, as are expenditures by candidates on their own behalf. These groups, which call themselves independent, have only one requirement: that their actions not be directed by the candidate or the candidate's staff. So a committee that is "independent" can maintain a veneer of aloofness from candidates for president or the Senate or the House and spend as much as it wants. The "independent committees" are all too obviously not that independent, and that provision of the Court's ruling increasingly is causing massive abuses. In addition, the Court's lack of any limitations on the candidate's personal spending is an invitation to millionaires simply to buy office—and this is exactly what many are doing. Some of our finest public officials are millionaires, but the ability to buy an office simply by dipping into your personal wealth is offensive.

One other item of interest: the 1982 congressional campaigns cost more than $300 million. The last British parliamentary election cost slightly more than $3 million.

What can be done about the campaign contribution mess? I am not optimistic that anything will be done until there is a scandal of major proportions, one the public can understand. The present situation, though sufficiently scandalous, is too complicated to be easily understood by the public. When a state auditor in Illinois stole more than $2 million, the story made headlines but did not seem to concern the electorate. When Illinois Governor William G. Stratton redecorated his office and bought a ninety-dollar wastebasket, however, the public outcry was overwhelming! People may not comprehend a $2 million scandal, but a ninety-dollar wastebasket they can. We now need a ninety-dollar wastebasket type of scandal with campaign contributions—something so clear-cut that everyone will be able to understand the sickness of the present system. In the meantime, incumbents tend to view the process that elected them, the process that gives them more in campaign contributions than their opponents, as ipso facto good.

We need a system of public financing, with strict limitations on what can be contributed and spent beyond those public funds. Representative David Obey of Wisconsin has introduced a bill that would be a workable experiment. But it must be an experiment only; there will be some flaws in what is tried, but even a flawed experiment will be an improvement over the present system. The ideal bill for House races would, according to my preferences:

- limit total expenditures to perhaps $200,000;
- limit personal and family expenditures to $20,000 (this is in the Obey proposal);
- limit Political Action Committee money to a total of $25,000, no more than $2,000 from any one committee;
- match money for small contributions up to $90,000 (in the Obey proposal);
- double that for any candidate whose opponent does not agree voluntarily to abide by these limitations (in the Obey proposal);
- make $15,000 available to each candidate to purchase radio and television time, with all other time, except free time available for debates, prohibited. Stations should be required to make commercials available in five-minute slots only, so that the slick, packaged thirty-second commercial could no longer be a factor;
- make free mail distribution available to any candidate attacked by an "independent committee" through the mails;
- have a mailing to each household in the district paid by the federal government with a five hundred word-statement by each candidate, plus brief biographical data. A candidate could state what his or her platform is, but would not be permitted to attack an opponent in this mailing.

There are problems with independent committees that this proposal would not solve. There is some indication that the Supreme Court may modify the independent-committee loophole. If necessary, I would even favor a constitutional amendment to deal with the problem, though I hope that would not be required.

The experiments with public financing in our states are too limited to provide conclusions. The Commonwealth of Puerto Rico has had the most experience with public funding, primarily supporting the established political parties, as is the case in several countries. The Scandinavian nations provide party support on the basis of the number of seats held in their respective Parliaments. West Germany, Great Britain, Canada, Israel, and Italy are among the nations with some sort of public financing. Almost all countries with public financing permit a limited amount of private financing. *I can find no example of a nation that has tried public financing and is considering going back to the days of total private support.*

Nothing evokes more spontaneous mail than Congress giving itself a pay raise. Though I have generally voted against pay raises (keeping my eye more on my electorate than the national good, I'm afraid), in 1982 I voted for one. *Time* magazine commented: "Congressional pay raises are long overdue; salaries have risen only 5.5% to $60,662, in the past five years, while the cost of living rose 62%."[21]

I am required to maintain two homes and I now have two children in college. In 1981 my net worth dropped about twenty thousand dollars, not counting inflation. We live comfortably in part because I write books, lecture for a fee, and have a small investment income. Some of the best members of the House and Senate have left in recent years for financial reasons. This statistical table shows part of the problem:

Category	Years Spanned	Percent Increase
CPI (Cost of Living)	1971–1981	124.6
Executives:		
Aerospace	1971–1981	1,000.1
Retailing	1971–1981	161.2
Banking	1971–1981	127.5
Advertising	1971–1981	94.6
Production Workers	1969–1982	158.4
White collar	1969–1982	155.0
Members of Congress	1971–1981	42.7[22]

If you take the top officers of the five hundred largest corporations in the United States and compare their salaries with the members of Congress and the cabinet, Congress and the cabinet would be at the bottom. Yet we run a business that has a budget fourteen times larger than the worldwide General Motors budget— and our "corporation" has life-and-death power over the other five hundred corporations, and makes decisions that help determine the destiny of civilization. The job should attract the finest, and in many ways it does. But the top people in the Los Angeles sanitation department receive higher salaries than do U.S. senators. A senior pilot for any major airline receives substantially more, as does the average physician and the average professional athlete. The May 30, 1983, issue of *U.S. News and World Report* published a survey of 327 of the largest U.S. corporations, looking at the salaries of 916 top officers of those companies. Salaries ranged from $98,846 for the lowest-paid vice-presidents to $2,544,495. The median salary for these 916 officers was $365,000—more than five times the salary of a U.S. senator.

To people trying to get by on Social Security, the salaries we receive look immense, and we should not receive so much that we lose touch with those who have to struggle to provide food and shelter. Where to draw that line is not easy.

The abler members of Congress and the cabinet can make substantially more money in other fields. That is as it should be. But when your financial situation causes you to borrow from your banker, and then you receive an offer to do something paying three times as much (your spouse gently reminding you that life outside Congress would mean shorter hours and less pressure), it makes you pause and think.

If the salaries of the members were doubled, to approximately the salary of the Japanese Diet—to use a hypothetical case I do not favor—would we attract better legislators and keep more of our able members? My instinct is that we would, that it would amount to only the smallest fraction of a percent in a federal budget and would improve the end product. A doubling of salary is not under consideration nor should it be, because of the public offense it would cause. But there is a problem. A newspaper in my district editorially blasted the most recent pay raise, saying there would be no shortage of people to run for Congress without it. That is correct, but the editorial totally missed the point. The question is what impact does a pay increase have on the *quality* of membership.

When I was serving in the General Assembly of Illinois a pay increase came up for consideration and, as always, provoked emotional debate. One of those who spoke against it said, "If you vote for this pay raise you're going to be attracting some able people to look at this office and run against you next time. Some of you won't come back." He was right. His speech against the pay raise was a powerful argument for it. The caliber of the Illinois General Assembly has gradually risen. How much that has to do with the substantial increases in salary that have been voted in recent years I do not know, but there is no question that salary is part of it.

A related issue is that of the honorarium, a fee for speaking to a convention or a college or some other group. The most basic requirement is being met, that it be disclosed; the public then can make its own judgment. Beyond that it is difficult to draw guidelines. The House has a dollar limitation, the Senate has just adopted one. I once was asked to speak to a large meeting of one of the major oil companies to explain why I opposed their stand. The fee was a thousand dollars, and I could have in good conscience accepted it. But I knew it would not look good in my disclosure at the end of the year, so I declined. The disclosure requirement probably is an adequate safeguard at this point, not only for what is improper, but for what appears to be improper.

There is one other money question that bothers me. In George McGovern's 1977 autobiography, *Grassroots*, he wrote: "My parents would be appalled by the extravagance of my upper-middle-class life style. And while not seeking to give it up, I myself am uneasy about it."[23] Jerry Voorhis, another former legislator, born to comfort, noted the economic problems of his friends as he grew up and recalled: "I had a sense of guilt whenever I was well dressed. I deliberately scuffed new shoes and crumpled new suits. I hated to wear an overcoat, knowing that many people had none."[24]

The question of relative wealth and the responsibilities that go with it has always troubled me, though perhaps not enough. The room in which I am typing this manuscript contains a television set, a stereo system, and heat emanating from a system that does not even require me to lift a finger. In the next room are a refrigerator and an electric range, and on the street is a 1980 Chevrolet, one of two cars my wife and I own. Tonight I will sleep between clean sheets in a comfortable bed. Although this may not be considered luxurious to some, compared to what more than 90 percent of the people of the world have, it is.

What is my moral responsibility—not simply as a member of Congress, but as a citizen—as it relates to all of this relative affluence? There are those who say there can be only one answer: abstain from these luxuries. I respect those who live by such convictions, but that solution troubles me, in part probably because I have become accustomed to certain comforts. But it is more than that. When I was a boy (I am fifty-four at this writing), I did not see wall-to-wall carpeting anywhere, or air conditioning, or electricity on many farms, or many of the things we now accept as part of normal life. I believe I could return to that more simple life and still be happy, but as a societal answer it falls short in two respects: first, if I abstain from the luxuries of television and carpeting, for example, I will have taken an isolated path that few others will follow, and the main impact probably will be that someone working in a television factory or a rug factory gets a little less work, as will the person in the retail outlet. The only good I would do, other than perhaps salving my own conscience, would come through the transfer of the income to some other cause. My second concern is this solution suggests that to raise the standard of living of those less fortunate there must be massive sacrifices on the part of the people of our country and other wealthy countries. If that were necessary, I would be pleased to do it. But it is not. In the last fifty years the standard of living of virtually all U.S. citizens has been raised appreciably. There is no reason that the worldwide standard of living cannot also be increased significantly for all, but that does require a sharing, a sharing of the growth in income that we will experience. Theologian Reinhold Niebuhr wrote: "A simple Christian morality counsels men to be unselfish. A profounder Christian faith must encourage men to create systems of justice which will save society and themselves from their own selfishness."[25] I do not want to be the affluent American eating too much while others starve, the man who takes a long, hot shower while others have no water, the man who is pampered medically while one and a half billion people have no medical services. If we were, however, to take but a small fraction of what we now spend on arms to help lift the lot of humanity, or if we were to follow the example of some of our friends in other countries (such as the Netherlands) in devoting a larger percentage of our economic growth to helping those in difficulty, the festering economic wounds many experience could begin to heal.

The United Nations Development Program, designed to help the world's poorest people, was created at the suggestion of the United States, and by tradition a U.S. citizen serves as its administrator. Contributions by each government are voluntary. There are some interesting statistics for donations made in 1982 (on a per-citizen basis): the United States contributed $0.56 per capita; Norway, $13.49; Denmark, $7.67; Sweden, $6.42; Switzerland, $2.74; Canada, $1.75; and Great Britain, $0.76. Many others—including the Soviet Union—do even worse than we do. But the myth that the United States outshines other nations in helping the world's poor is exactly that: a myth. In total development assistance, under all programs, the United States provides approximately $25 per capita; Great Britain, $39; West German, $51; France, $77; the Netherlands, Sweden, and Norway, $100.

Comfort in a world of poverty is obviously a dilemma almost all citizens face, not only the office holder. I am troubled by having more than others have, in part because I see no national vision by our leaders that would move us to help those in distress. Our people yearn for such leadership, leadership that would appeal to the nobler instincts in each of us.

How we use money will determine whether people live or die. How we control the use of money in campaigns will determine who shapes that policy.

☆ 5 ☆

The Dilemma of Time

You may ask for anything you like except time.
        —Napoleon, to one of his officers[1]

I wasted time, and now doth time waste me.
        —King Richard in Shakespeare's
        King Richard II[2]

W hen the moral dilemmas of politics are discussed, most people think in terms of money or political pressures; but for many in the House and Senate the greater dilemma is how to parcel out time.

The extra five minutes spent by a legislator in understanding a problem or promoting an idea could have a positive impact on national policy. The seed planted in that five minutes could grow for the nation. Perhaps an extra few minutes should be spent studying a bill or an amendment. Maybe the three minutes I take to make a phone call for a constituent or a community will solve a problem. Effective legislators are those who manage to squeeze a maximum amount of activity into the limited time we all have. After almost a year as president, John F. Kennedy said, "We must use time as a tool, not as a couch. We must serve our own destiny."[3]

Although there are many things that can be handled as well tomorrow as today, next year as this year, for those who are hungry or unemployed or in great need, how long it takes Congress to act—or the person representing them in Congress to act—can make a difference not only in the quality of life, but also in whether or not life goes on. Former member Jerry Voorhis recalls that the urgency of the problems facing people "can drive a member to distraction. It did me."⁴ Pushing research on cystic fibrosis *now* (a problem I am working on as I write this book) is important because the National Institutes of Health will make a decision within the next few days that may well determine how soon the disease is conquered, how long some people may live, whether those struggling with this killer can have some hope. I cannot sit back leisurely and wait for some convenient time to act. How much should I listen to lobbyists, who may be experts in their field but usually represent a special, moneyed interest? In the midst of weighty discussions about the threat of nuclear war, I suddenly find myself working on a problem about a parking place for my staff; how can I avoid that kind of petty detail? In every political campaign the manager asks the candidate to spend more time on the telephone raising money; is this the way I should be spending my time? Should I be pushing Congress to adjourn early (and leave problems unmet) so I can spend more time back in the district where my opponent is campaigning, undeterred by a congressional session?

Even more serious is the whole question of arms control. Each day that passes without a significant arms control agreement pushes the world, by some small immeasurable distance, one day closer to destruction. Each day more and more weapons are built, the ability to destroy ourselves grows, and the odds increase that at some point self-restraint will not guide the decision of a world leader. Unless we recognize the urgency of weapons control, that time is our enemy not our friend, we court disaster.

How should I divide my time between Washington and my home district? In Washington how much time should I spend on individual problems of my constituents and their communities and how much time should I spend with my family? How much time do I need simply to relax and unwind, to play tennis, work in the yard, take a vacation? How can I use my time effectively so that I don't become too narrow in focus, so that I bring a broad enough perspective to my work? Writing helps me to refine my thinking (and helps pay the mortgage), but how much of it should I do? What books should I read?

These and a host of other time-related questions are among the most difficult a member of Congress has to face.

The problem of effective use of time is not new to public officials. Edward Gibbon, in his famous history of the Roman Empire, noted that the fourth-century emperor Julian "considered every moment as lost that was not devoted to the advantage of the public or the improvement of his own mind. By this avarice of time he seemed to protract the short duration of his reign; and, if the dates were less securely ascertained, we should refuse to believe that only sixteen months elapsed between the death of Contantinius and the departure of his successor for the Persian war."[5]

A less wholesome example is provided by the father of modern history, Herodotus (c. 450 B.C.), who reports that Mycerinus, king of Egypt, was advised by an oracle he had only six years to live. The king, "perceiving that his doom was fixed, had lamps prepared, which he lighted every day at eventime, and feasted and enjoyed himself both day and night. . . . His wish was to prove the oracle false, by turning the nights into days, and so living twelve years in the space of six."[6]

There are times when as a member of Congress I feel I am also trying to squeeze two days into one. Here is a fairly typical day's schedule. I get up at 7:00, leave for work about 7:45, and in the evening leave for home between 7:00 and 7:30. I take home reports and material that I did not have time to read during the day. Two or three times a week after I leave the office I attend some type of meeting before going home. Some evenings we have night sessions. During the day I have two or three committee meetings (often conflicting in time, presenting its own set of dilemmas); I see several constituents, federal officials, and staff members; I sign fifty to a hundred letters and dictate others; I vote on issues before the House and on some days participate in debate; I meet with two or three reporters and talk to six more on the phone; I read at least three newspapers; I plow through some of the material my staff believes is important or that interests me particularly. I spend more time on the phone than I like. (Eleanor Roosevelt once told me she had a policy of handling almost everything by correspondence rather than by telephone or personal appointment. "Many people want to see you and talk to you when they could just as easily handle these matters by correspondence."[7])

The person who handles my scheduling, Vicki Coupling, does an excellent job of screening the people I should see and those with whom others on the staff should meet. I keep visits to my office brief; most people can say in five minutes what they would prefer to say in fifteen. I walk fast, saving myself a few minutes every day. There are perhaps twenty small things I do each day to save a little more time. One such activity, unwisely, is eating fast. The late Senator Richard Neuberger of Oregon made it a point to eat with others so that he would not eat too rapidly. I frequently join others for a meal, saving my stomach a little wear and tear. If all of that sounds a bit hectic and frantic, I am comforted by the words of De Lawd in *Green Pastures*: "Even bein' God ain't no bed of roses."

It is ironic that in the midst of all this activity the public still has the impression the Congress "isn't doing anything." I don't know whether this is because the public sees problems not getting solved, or because of snatches of news items they read or see or hear, or if it is like some distant airplane that appears to be standing still but is actually traveling at six hundred miles an hour.

I have not been able to convince all my constituents that I use my time either fully or wisely. Once, in the midst of a particularly long and gueling day, I received the following note from an unhappy constituent:

> Dear Congressman P. Simon
>   You have been in office some time now and have done absululy nothing. But set on your can and get a big fat Government paycheck. or maybe you don't know what to do. so I'll give you a list of thing we want done yesterday.

It is not likely that I will ever convince this constituent of the contributions of my tenure in office!

I had another complaint from a gentleman I had greeted briefly during a visit he made to Washington. He told me later that my predecessor had taken two hours to show him around the Capitol and had assigned a staff person to drive him around Washington, while I had only spent five minutes with him. This man was not pleased with my use of time, and if my sole criterion is what pleases the constituents back home, then I ought to spend more time being hospitable. I don't want to appear brusque. There is much truth to Tennyson's words: "The greater man, the greater courtesy."[8] But time I take as a host and guide diminishes the impact I can have on national legislation or problems in my district. The solution to this dilemma is not difficult for me, though it may not necessarily be politically astute.

Until I recently became a candidate for the U.S. Senate, I spent at least every other weekend in the district, plus a portion of the time Congress is not in session. One of the most effective uses of time in the district is what we call open office hours. I go to a village hall (or a store or in a very small community a home) for perhaps two hours. Notice is given in advance that I will be there, and then people line up and I see them one at a time about a Social Security check that is missing, what they think about our China policy, or whatever else is on their minds. I have been to virtually every community in my district and it helps me to keep in touch with people's problems.

Time constraints cause special dangers in geographically large districts. Because time is so important, private plane travel is frequently necessary. As a result, for several years one of the leading causes of death among House members was airplane accidents. I try to provide some protection for myself by using caution about who flies me and by insisting on two motors and two pilots.

Receptions and dinners cause another time problem, one I have solved: I rarely go to them. I write a weekly column for the newspapers in my district, and in my third year in the House I wrote:

Thanks, but No Thanks
This day's mail is like most others: nine invitations to receptions around Washington. In this morning's mail I have a letter from a labor union unhappy because I didn't show up at their reception.

When I first came to Washington, I tried to drop in briefly at many receptions and dinners. But I soon discovered that I couldn't afford the expenditure of time.

I like people as much as anyone does. I enjoy visiting. But it became obvious that while it was pleasant visiting, little of a constructive nature was being accomplished.

So I started suggesting to people who invited me to receptions that, rather than my going to their cocktail parties, they drop by my office for a ten-minute chat about whatever interested them. . . .

So don't feel insulted if I don't accept your invitation if you belong to the Lumber Dealers or the Real Estate Association or the Carpenters Union or the Mental Health Society or any one of the thousands (literally) of groups which hold receptions. . . . I serve the people of my district best, and the people of the nation best, by digging into the issue papers and mail which accumulate on my desk, rather than digging into some caviar and sipping drinks you pay for.

And let me add a word to the various organizations: My guess is that most other members of Congress feel as I do. They would sooner have you save your money and drop into their offices where more substantial conversation can take place. . . .

That does not mean that I won't go to dinner with a friend, nor am I saying that I will never again go to a reception. . . .

Right now I have a pile of mail on my desk that accumulated during the days when I visited the district. I have information on various subjects that my staff believes I should at least glance through—and it's piled up more than one foot in height.

Should I leave all of that to visit one or two of a half dozen receptions going on tonight?

The right answer, for me at least, is no.

I attend events at which I feel I can learn something or to which I can contribute, and those I think I'll enjoy. One week, for example, I attended an evening meeting where the late Buckminister Fuller, then an eighty-seven-year-old man with fresh ideas, talked to about fifteen of us in the House about his sense of the future. Another evening I met with some Jesuit priests at Georgetown University, where they recorded some dialogues.

Both were worth the time. On those occasions I missed thirty to forty other events.

Perhaps it appears that I don't enjoy my work. On the contrary, I do. But like other legislators, I find myself involved in a series of time struggles, aware that I can never completely achieve any of the goals I have set. But how effectively I use my time may determine whether we obtain money for a sewer system in my district, or whether I get something done as practical— and usually much needed—as shining my shoes, or move some small measure toward eliminating unemployment or achieving arms control.

There is satisfaction in using time for a noble goal, in feeling that life is not wasted. "A man who has never lost himself in a cause bigger than himself has missed one of life's mountaintop experiences," Richard Nixon said.[9] I believe that. But political observer Elizabeth Drew is also correct when she writes that increasingly we are governed by "politicians who are exhausted, who can't think clearly, who don't think about broad questions— don't have the time, even if they have the inclination to do so."[10]

My children are now twenty-two and nineteen, and both are in college. They grew up in the political milieu, and they understood the demands of my job. But it still was not pleasant to hear them sometimes say as I left home carrying a suitcase, "Are you going away *again?*" There are pluses, of course, as well as minuses for political families. The children get to visit the White House and meet many whose names are familiar to the nation. When my daughter, Sheila, was perhaps thirteen years old, my wife and I saw her busily engaged in a conversation with Senator George McGovern at a small dinner party we attended. When I asked Sheila afterward what she and McGovern had been talking about, she replied, "He was explaining Watergate to me." That was an experience she is not likely to forget. When my son, Martin, was ten years old, we hosted a luncheon for Walter Mondale, then a United States senator. As Mondale went through the food line at the buffet, my wife and I talked about who might sit next to him, planning to give that honor to some local official or political leader. But before we could work it out, we looked over and saw that Martin had selected the spot next to the future vice-president, and both appeared to be having a good time. Martin recalls that with pleasure.

Occasionally, we are able to combine political interests and family interests. Congressman Stephen Neal of North Carolina had been sending letters to his congressional colleagues about saving the New River, threatened by the construction of a huge hydroelectric dam. The facts as he presented them intrigued me, so our family canoed down the New River. It gave me firsthand information about a problem facing Congress and at the same time provided a good experience for the family. Not so incidentally, congressional action rescued the New River.

When the children were younger I reserved at least one week each year for a vacation and I blocked out certain weekends to be with the family. As they became teenagers they developed their own schedules, which meant less time with them. I promised both my daughter and son that before they graduate from college I would take each on a trip abroad. I invited my daughter, then a senior at Wittenberg University in Ohio, to join me over the 1982 Christmas–New Year's holiday on a trip to Italy, Germany, Hungary, and the Soviet Union. She was studying Russian, so it would give her a chance to practice. When the time came for us to leave Washington, there were still several votes pending in a special session of Congress, and as I deliberated whether to cancel the trip or skip those votes, I chatted with Representative Bruce Vento of Minnesota. He said, "I know what I'd do. I'd go." He gave me sound advice . . . and I took it.

People in many occupations share the dilemma of how much time to devote to family, how much to the job, how much to church and other activities. Members of the House and Senate hear frequently from their spouses: "You are married to your job and not to me"—a valid criticism. Like many fathers, if I were to retrace my steps I would probably spend a little more time with my family and lengthen that vacation a bit. The voters in my district want that from me as well as conscientious service on the job.

What books should I take the time to read? Novels do not interest me, though, somewhat inconsistently, I enjoy a good movie, also a work of fiction. I have a pile of books on my nightstand, and most nights I read a little from two or three of them. More than a century ago John Stuart Mill observed that human beings cease striving for noble goals "as they lose their intellectual tastes."[11] It is important, both for diversion and for perspective, for a member of Congress to read outside his or her "field": a history of Greece, an article on the arts, a study of architecture. There is no such thing as having too much knowledge. I have just finished reading a book about the death of Napoleon (the author argues that he was murdered). I learned a little about Napoleon, a little about wine and arsenic, a little geography. I cannot tell you that it will ever help me in my job as a legislator, but in a way I cannot measure I have been enriched by reading it. We need to stretch our minds, get away from tomorrow's amendments and next week's budget votes. We need to escape the truism: "The trouble with the world is that the man of thought doesn't act and the man of action doesn't think."[12]

Humanity operates on a "nature abhors a vacuum" theory, assuming that if someone with a right answer does not move on a situation someone with a wrong answer will. Usually that is correct. But there are times when frantic activity is not the right answer, when wounds need to heal. I recall when the chairman of the Education and Labor Committee, Representative Carl Perkins of Kentucky, talked to me about holding off a vote on the House floor on an important measure that had deeply divided the committee before it received a favorable committee vote. "Let's let things cool off a little," he said. Time can be a healer. Shakespeare has Iago counsel: "How poor are they that have not patience! What wound did ever heal but by degrees?"[13]

Time is also a factor when deciding issues on which victory will not be achieved soon. We as a society favor quick solutions, whether it be in the form of a TV dinner or religious conversion during a thirty-minute television show. Things have to happen *now*. Introduce a proposal on an issue that will not affect us immediately, but on which discussion should begin today if the proper steps are ever to be taken, and reporters will ask you if you believe the measure has a chance of passage in this session. If you say no, they ask you why you introduced it. The long-range implications seem inadequate in our high-speed society. The politically opportune thing to do is to avoid such long-range issues. We look for legislation that can pass quickly and have equally rapid and visible results; we ought to be looking much more at the long-range picture. Historian Will Durant has written: "From barbarism to civilization requires a century; from civilization to barbarism needs but a day."[14]

There is another dilemma related to time, one in which the public helps to make the decisions: how long a House or Senate member should serve.

As an opponent of the automatic seniority system in Congress, I might be expected to applaud the turnover in House and Senate membership. There are those whose retirement I do applaud, but there are others who have retired who could still be contributing much to the nation. Some retire for financial reasons; others are simply tired of the pressures; some feel they have grown stale on the job; and others retire for health or age reasons.

But the turnover has been more rapid than it should be. In the early 1700s Thomas Parnell wrote in one of his poems: "Let time, that makes you homely, make you a sage."[15] In one of the *Dialogues*, Plato has a citizen of Crete say to an old Athenian: "You see with the keen vision of age."[16] Wisdom often does come with years and with experience. Representative George Mahon of Texas, who retired from the House at the age of seventy-nine, quietly moved around the Capitol building, with few visitors recognizing him or understanding his influence. He served as chairman of the House Appropriations Committee. His voting record was more conservative than mine, but any member of the House or Senate will tell you he made a tremendous contribution to the nation. At the age of seventy-nine many people should retire. In his case, retirement meant a loss to the nation.

Although Aristotle advocated restricting tenure in office to six months, arbitrary rules should not be set. Those with both age and wisdom should be listened to in the halls of the nation's Capitol. We do not need to reinvent the wheel every ten years; we do not need to make the same mistakes over and over again. Whether a representative or senator has reached the point of wisdom or dotage is a judgment voters must make.

The dilemmas of time are with those of us who serve in public office, and with those who select public officials.

☆ 6 ☆

Inappropriate Responses to World Hunger and the Nuclear Threat

> Hey, hey Woody Guthrie, I wrote you a song 'bout a funny
> ol' world that's a-comin' along.
> Seems sick an' it's hungry, it's tired and it's torn,
> It looks like it's a-dyin' an' it's hardly been born.
> —Bob Dylan[1]

> The risks inherent in disarmament pale in comparison to the
> risks inherent in an unlimited arms race. It is therefore our
> intention to challenge the Soviet Union, not to an arms race,
> but to a peace race—to advance with us step by step, stage
> by stage, until general and complete disarmament has actually
> been achieved . . .
> —John F. Kennedy, 1961[2]

> The fact that the coercive factor in society is both necessary
> and dangerous seriously complicates the whole task of se-
> curing both peace and justice.
> —Reinhold Niebuhr[3]

There are no issues in which the morally desirable goals are clearer than the elimination of involuntary hunger and the creation of a world of peace. Reaching those goals involves such a complex series of issues that most people feel overwhelmed and regard them as a distant dream they can do nothing about. That is the first major obstacle. The second obstacle is that, though the ultimate goals are supported by everyone, the steps necessary to achieve them are not particularly popular.

Complexity is a defense mechanism everyone uses on some issues from time to time. It has limited validity. For example, I know nothing about automobiles, so I take my car to someone who does. There is no need for me to waste my time learning about carburetors, distributor caps, or fuel pumps. The danger with making that conscious or subconscious analogy to issues of world hunger and peace is that in the case of the car my relative inattention to the matter does not prevent the car from being fixed. On the issues of hunger and peace, inattention breeds starvation and an arms race. The legislator or citizen who through inattention displays indifference to these two issues takes a morally reprehensible posture. Decent people do not commit murder; but, comfortably sealed off from the world's miseries and potential calamities, that is precisely what they do. More than a century ago someone observed: "It sometimes happens that he who would not hurt a fly will hurt a nation."⁴ Good, decent members of Congress, who would share their meal with a hungry person if that person came to them, will vote to deny food to millions of the hungry apparently without realizing what they are doing. A World War II veteran once told me: "After my infantry duty I got transferred to the air corps. I found it much easier to drop bombs on cities than to aim a gun at a man."⁵ The bomber depersonalized the deaths, even though there were many more of them. Indifference to the arms race or world hunger is not as visibly offensive as ignoring a person on a sidewalk screaming for help. Indifference is easy because it is depersonalized, but it is devastating.

That is not to suggest that a specific course of conduct will be immediately clear on these issues. Concerned people will—and do—differ on the proper approach. Legislators and citizens do not always make the right choice, but if the comfortable but dangerous veneer of indifference could be shed, this nation and the world would make substantial strides, not toward a utopia, but toward a world with much less misery, a world much less threatened by self-destruction.

Indifference is not the only obstacle, however. For not only are the issues complicated, but frequently the paths toward achievement of these laudable goals are unpopular.

Some issues, such as preserving our gradually depleting topsoil so food can be grown, produce thunderous yawns. Others evoke active hostility. Not many years ago the United States had a substantial malnutrition problem among the poor. The nation inaugurated a food assistance program. Independent studies have since shown that despite deficiencies in the program the food stamps (and the commodity program that preceded it), together with school lunches, have virtually eliminated severe malnutrition among this nation's poor. History will show food stamps to be one of the better programs our government has undertaken. Yet if you were to take a poll among my constituents, a relatively poor rural district, the votes would be overwhelmingly in favor of abolishing the program. Most of the abuses of the food stamp program we hear about either have been eliminated through changes in the law or are violations of the law. The *maximum* food stamp benefit is seventy cents per person per meal for a family for four, not exactly a lobster and champagne diet. Nevertheless, we still hear stories about people who use food stamps to buy steaks, lobster, and Pepsi-Cola. There *are* some imprudent purchases with food stamps, for one of the reasons people are poor is that they make bad judgments, even about the food they buy. But for well over 90 percent of the recipients the food stamp program is an essential tool for preventing hunger, not a chance for abuse. Unfortunately, food stamps have become an easy target for budget cutters in the House and Senate who want to play the role of demagogue. (Sentor Bob Dole of Kansas is one of the major exceptions; he has been a courageous defender of food stamps.) It's easy to go back home and make speeches against food stamps, because even the recipients want to stop the abuses; but for the poor, more than half of whom are children, those stamps provide the difference between an adequate diet and malnutrition.

Similarly, school lunches have become easy prey. Anyone involved can tell you about the waste of food, which is real. But in the first two Reagan years, Congress "reformed" the school lunch program so that more than three million young people in our schools no longer receive them. Interestingly, the school lunch program did not originate with educators, who took the task on reluctantly, but with the Department of Defense. When we had the draft, far too many could not pass the physical, in large part because they had had an inadequate diet when they were young. The Defense Department suggestion for school lunches found a ready reception with the nation's farmers, who saw it as an opportunity to increase the demand and prices for food. Tests soon showed that when young people had one good meal a day—and many before that had not—they learned more in school. So a program designed originally to help the nation's security, and supported by agriculture, had to be defended by educators.[6] Now we have come full circle and presumably we will continue to lag in support of the program until the day when some generals and admirals point out once again that something is wrong with the young men and women taking the military's physicals.

When people are asked what federal expenditures should be cut, foreign economic assistance programs rank at the top of the unpopular list. But poll the same people on whether we should help starving people in Africa or anywhere else, and they will overwhelmingly say yes. This presents one of the fundamental choices public figures face, on this and other issues: *Do you appeal to people on the basis of fear and selfishness, or do you appeal to their finer instincts?*

There is the base, as well as the good, in all of us. That observation reflects the Judeo-Christian view of humanity, which recognizes the flaws in all of us. Politically, it is easier to appeal to the selfish rather than the noble; it is easier to stir fear and a "look out for number one" attitude than it is the positive and constructive forces within each of us.

Foreign economic assistance is a good issue on which to form a partial judgment of a member of the House and Senate. I do not say that a member casts an immoral vote if he or she opposes foreign economic assistance. I have known some to vote against an authorization or appropriation simply because they regarded it as woefully inadequate. There is also more military assistance in these programs than there should be, and some legislators vote against the measure because of that. Sometimes there is not enough emphasis on helping the miserably poor within recipient countries. But if a legislator stands before an audience and says, "Let's stop sending money to other countries; let's spend it on our own problems," it is likely that he or she is using a convenient and surefire way to get votes, one that ignores the long-range best interests of the nation. That type of candidate or official usually also opposes spending money to solve domestic problems.

In July 1976 Dr. John Hannah, former president of Michigan State University and once chairman of the U.S. Civil Rights Commission, told a small group: "I'm seventy-four years old. I see this task of meeting the world's food needs as the most important task which the world has to face, but surprisingly there aren't many young people interested."[7] The situation has not worsened since that time, but it has not improved much either.

Approximately eight hundred million of the earth's four and a half billion people face severe malnutrition, and millions more receive the most minimally adequate diet. "Food, glorious food" are the first three words of a pleasant song from the musical *Oliver*. For much of the earth, however, those three words represent a haunting dream. The richest 20 percent of the world's population consumes 71 percent of the world's food and industrial production; the poorest 20 percent consumes 2 percent of it. Approximately one-fourth of the people who die each year are below the age of five. In many countries the leading causes of death are diarrhea, whooping cough, measles—diseases either minor or almost forgotten here. Rarely is death listed as simple starvation. But the nutritional level is so low a disease that would barely be noticed by a healthy, well-nourished person kills the already weakened. Almost all of this is preventable. The earth does not lack the resources, it lacks the will.

Indifference to that is immoral.

In the arms race we face the possibility of the extinction of humanity. It is that simple. We can create a world in which never again will the cry of a baby be heard, a deer be seen, a blade of grass be grown. In *The Fate of the Earth*, Jonathan Schell notes that the world's nuclear warheads today contain 1,600,000 times the destructive power of the first bomb that fell on Hiroshima. Schell adds: "We have thus far failed to fashion, or to discover within ourselves, an emotional or intellectual or political response [to that awesome reality]."[8] Year after year it gets worse. Since World War II the efficiency of the average U.S. car (fuel use to weight) has doubled, and in that same time the efficiency of nuclear weapons (destructive yield to weight) has increased 150 times.[9] We are stockpiling more and more of these increasingly powerful warheads. "We are," said Admiral Hyman G. Rickover after his retirement, "in danger of arming ourselves into oblivion."[10]

The two superpowers have not shown an adequate interest in making headway on this problem, despite lip service to the contrary. In the last few years the Soviets have taken a more positive public stance than the United States, but in the conventional arms-reduction talks in Vienna they have shown no inclination to accept any proposals that would reduce forces and tensions. The Soviets have been unwilling—perhaps because of a lack of understanding of how the U.S. system works—to take action in the field of human rights that would create a better climate within which our public officials can operate. The Soviet action in Afghanistan increased tensions, as did the U.S. invasion of Grenada. The United States has been far from blameless. Salt II was not approved by the U.S. Senate after it had been negotiated by Presidents Ford and Carter. President Reagan not only indicated hostility to Salt II (though he is abiding by its terms, as are the Soviets), but he has also taken the stand that since the Soviets are ahead militarily—an inaccurate generalization—the United States has to build up its defenses before we can negotiate successfully. As we build our defenses, so the theory goes, the Soviets would have to do likewise, but they would be so hurt economically that they would either call a halt to the arms race or their economic system would collapse. In 1981, Secretary of State Alexander Haig, eager to please Reagan and at that time all too obviously hoping to become a Republican candidate for president, enthusiastically endorsed this notion of the imminent collapse of the Soviet system, much to the embarrassment of our friends in Western Europe and around the world. Further increasing tensions, the president said the Soviets "have openly and publicly declared that the only morality they recognize is what will further their cause, meaning they reserve unto themselves the right to commit any crime, to lie, to cheat, in order to attain that, and that is moral, not immoral, and we operate on a different set of standards."[11] In 1983 President Reagan told a convention of the National Association of Evangelicals that the

Soviet Union is the "focus of evil in the modern world."[12] The danger with this stance is that if we view others as evil, we are by implication good. Almost any action by the good to stamp out the evil can appear justified. Hitler convinced enough Germans that the Jews represented evil, and repeated it enough, so that any response to the Jews seemed justified. Saint Augustine provided good advice on this score: "Never fight evil as if it arose totally outside of yourself."[13] Historian Henry Steele Commager called this particular Reagan speech "the worst presidential speech in American history,"[14] a hasty judgment in a contest in which there could be many entrants.

The U.S. attitude toward both military and moral realities has numerous weaknesses. While Reagan views the Soviet Union as an immoral nation, they see us as a morally inferior society characterized by *Playboy* magazine, violence, and an overemphasis on material goods. The Soviets are ahead in a few military categories and are stronger in certain geographical areas, but overall the United States is "ahead," if you can say either nation is ahead in a military race in which each side can completely destroy the other many times over. The idea that we will be able to amass more arms and weapons systems and improve our position assumes the Soviets will not do the same, a position history does not justify. I know of no Soviet expert who believes that. Finally, to base such a policy on the belief that the Soviet system will collapse contradicts the Central Intelligence Agency's estimate of the Soviet economic situation and flies in the face of the observations of most visitors to the USSR. The Soviet system has substantial flaws, does not work well, but it does work. The United States would be foolish to base our policy on any other assumption.

Living on the edge of total destruction through nuclear war is not good for a society. Historian Will Durant notes of an earlier period: "Never in known history had Englishmen (now so law-abiding) been so lawless. A hundred years of war had made men brutal and reckless."[15] We have seen the aftermath of the Korean and Vietnam wars in isolated incidents of violence—sometimes by returning veterans, sometimes by citizens accustomed to the steady drumbeat of violence. Something happens to all of us when bloodshed in living color is a regular staple of our television news. When a high percentage of high school students feel they will not live out a normal life span because the earth will be destroyed in a nuclear war, that sense of doom inevitably shapes conduct and attitudes in ways we cannot know or measure but that I fear cannot be good. A study of children in the Boston area showed that "even third-graders were aware of the possibility of nuclear war—far more aware than their parents knew—aware during the daytime and during their nightmares."[16]

A change in public concern on arms is evident. In 1960 J. Robert Oppenheimer, a leading nuclear scientist, noted: "I find myself profoundly anguished over the fact that no ethical discourse of any nobility or weight has been addressed to the problem of atomic weapons."[17] Yet in 1983 this nation's Roman Catholic bishops broke a tradition of vocal or silent support of U.S. military policy with a call to halt the nuclear arms race. Protestant and Jewish leaders have echoed that refrain.

The call for arms reduction expressed in the massive gathering of approximately 750,000 in New York City, as well as the November 1982 vote in scattered locations throughout the nation that called for a nuclear freeze, and the mounting pressure from Congress for the administration to move on arms control—all these have caused some perceptible shift on the part of President Reagan. He and Soviet Secretary Andropov could make themselves history's heroes if they were to make significant headway on arms reduction. It is one of those rare circumstances when the applause of today's crowds would be echoed in the acclaim of history.

Just as public opinion has caused at least something of a shift by the Reagan administration, so it can move lawmakers. Even Soviet leadership is not completely immune to public opinion, as their jamming of the Voice of America, Radio Free Europe, and Radio Liberty illustrates.

Although there is no question about the moral imperative for moving in the direction of an arms-control agreement, there are judgment calls on how to get there. The Reverend J. Bryan Hehir, a leading Roman Catholic spokesman, said: "There is no non-moral approach to policy and there cannot be a purely moral answer to policy questions."[18]

For example, I oppose the B-1 bomber construction as a sense-less waste of money that further escalates the arms race, but colleagues whom I respect feel the B-1 is essential to balance growing Soviet arms might. I would rather have the president come to Congress and say, "Please hold off building the B-1 bomber at this time. I'm gong to ask the Sovets to reduce their arms buildup in return for our abandoning the B-1. If we cannot reach agreement with the Soviets, I will be back," than have Congress kill the project. But since the president is unwilling to take that posture, my vote is for some restraint in arms buildup on our side, in the hope that this *may* result in some restraint and reevaluation by the Soviets—a gamble, but not much of one in view of the B-52 bomber strength, the Stealth bomber soon to emerge, and other means the United States has for delivering warheads. There is also some truth to the observation that "strength becomes weakness because of the vanity in strength."[19] Senator Richard Russell of Georgia said somewhat the same thing when he opposed creation of a U.S. rapid deployment force because he believed we would be too easily tempted to use it. Drawing the fine line between strength that is needed for the nation's security and strength that becomes destabilizing is not easy.

Politically, there is a gamble involved for legislators who refuse to vote for almost any arms increase. Such voting will cause a negative rating by the American Security Council, a group whose name belies the fact that they refuse to divulge their finances and are probably a front for defense contractors. It will cause a negative rating by groups like the Veterans of Foreign Wars, no matter how strongly the member supports services to veterans. And defense-related industries in a district or state are not en-thusiastic about such votes. A vote to cut any defense expenditure will generally result in more negative editorials than favorable ones, though that varies from district to district and state to state.

Historian Barbara W. Tuchman has written: "International policy is rarely guided by morality."[20] There are times, however, when morality is visible in the decision-making process. In an arms race, whether the motivation is moral or merely a selfish desire to survive, any move toward a world more likely to avoid nuclear holocaust is desirable. I am appreciably less interested in motivation (which is mixed, in all of us) than I am in the end result.

The difficulty with legislative and public concern about the nuclear threat is not only the inadequacy of its unfocused intensity, but that the concern now deals only with the dramatic surface issues while almost totally ignoring the more fundamental work that must be done.

We should be trying to build a much broader understanding between the Soviet Union and the United States in particular, and among nations in general. There has been a substantial increase in weapons strength and destructive power in the past two decades, but a decline in understanding. Some purists prefer that. In splendid isolation we can assume our moral superiority and their moral inferiority, uncluttered by the facts. Such artificial probity courts disaster. A visitor to the USSR is surprised at how little the Soviet people understand the United States. But my impression is that we are equally misunderstanding of them.

Yet we are doing virtually nothing to improve the situation. We now spend more money to construct a quarter mile of interstate highway than we do on all of our exchange programs with the Soviet Union and the other Warsaw Pact countries. Study of the Russian language is on the decrease. Twenty years ago there were forty-eight Minnesota high schools offering Russian courses; today there are three. In the last five years more than eighty U.S. colleges and universities have dropped Russian from their language programs. On campuses where Russian is still being taught interest is diminishing. I spoke recently at Michigan Technological University, a school that still teaches Russian; there are three students taking the course.

It is unlikely that the Soviets will send tanks into Central Europe, or that U.S. missiles will suddenly hit Soviet soil—though each nation genuinely fears these possibilities. A much more likely scenario, one that could lead to world destruction, is the escalation of a clash of interests in the Middle East or Latin America or some other region. To prevent that from happening, the United States works with other nations to keep any such situation from becoming too inflamed. But the best safeguard to such accidental escalation is U.S.–Soviet understanding, and unfortunately that safeguard has come close to disappearing at the very time it is most important.

This lack of understanding is illustrated by the 1983 *Newsweek* poll on the question "Who is more likely to initiate a nuclear attack in Europe, the United States or the Soviet Union?"[21] In the United States the answer was the Soviet Union 65–12 percent, with 23 percent uncertain. If the same poll were taken in the Soviet Union, the reverse probably would be true. What is of more than casual interest is the response among other Western powers to the same question: in France 49 percent thought the Soviet Union was the greater threat to peace and 11 percent thought the United States was, with 40 percent uncertain; in West Germany 45 percent said the Soviet Union and 20 percent the United States, with 35 percent uncertain; in the Netherlands the ratio was 31–20 percent, with 49 percent uncertain; and in Great Britain it was 48–28 percent, with 24 percent uncertain. Those are not statistics overwhelmingly in our favor. In each of these countries more than half the people either believe the United States is the greater threat or are uncertain as to which nation is the greater threat. We assume our country will not be the one to start a nuclear war (and I believe that), but this is less obvious to other Western democracies, much less to the leaders and people of the Soviet Union. We assume others understand us, when frequently their understanding of us is almost as bad as our understanding of them. When a wire service story quoted me as saying that people in both the Soviet Union and the United States want peace, I was startled by people who wrote assuring me that the Soviet citizens do not want peace, even citing the Bible to prove it. These people have never been to the Soviet Union. They have developed such strong opinions on the basis of speeches by public officials and religious leaders and what they have picked up from the media. I wish I could take these people to Leningrad, where more Soviets died during World War II than U.S. citizens over the course of World Wars I and II, the Korean War, and the Vietnam War. Although we should be wary of Sovet adventurism, the level of misunderstanding that now exists between our two nations should also be a major concern.

In a world where the United States ought to be trying to

understand other nations more, fewer and fewer faculty members from U.S. campuses study, teach, or travel abroad. We remain the only nation on the face of the earth in which you can go through elementary school, high school, college, and four years of graduate school without ever having had a year of a foreign language.*

During World War II an "I Am an American Day" rally was held in New York City's Central Park. One of the speakers, the distinguished jurist Learned Hand, said: "What then is the spirit of liberty? I cannot define it; I can only tell you my own faith. . . . The spirit of liberty is the spirit which seeks to understand the minds of other men and women; the spirit of liberty is the spirit which weighs their interests alongside its own without bias."[22] That willingness to seek out and undertand others has been languishing in this country.

Fulbright scholarships and other exchange programs have suffered a decline over the past decade—and the decline would have been even more precipitous had the Reagan administration had its way. Within the Department of Education, for example, the number of Fulbright Fellowships declined from 2,557 in 1970 to 828 in 1980, and the educational exchanges under the Mutual Educational and Cultural Exchange Act declined by one-third. The Reagan administration asked for a 60-percent cut beyond that in both programs. This is an irrational policy, whether your concern is for extending U.S. political influence or understanding the world. In virtually every part of the world, the Soviets now offer more scholarship opportunities than does the United States. At a 1982 high school commencement in Panama, leaflets were distributed to all graduating seniors, inviting them to a meeting where they could learn how to win scholarships to attend college in Moscow. There are no similar leaflets from the United States, nor as many opportunities here. In Central America and the Caribbean alone, for example, the Soviets provide more than five thousand full scholarships for attending college in the USSR. The United States provides 758. The Soviets are increasing their program, but we operate at less than 60 percent of our 1965

---

*For a discussion of the foreign-language problem, see *The Tongue-Tied American: Confronting the Foreign-Language Crisis*, by Paul Simon (New York: Continuum, 1980).

levels. And, unfortunately, the foreign students who come to the United States are increasingly the children of the wealthy or are from the wealthier nations.

Yet there is a yearning for better understanding between almost all people, even in those areas where there are long traditions of bitter rivalry.

The United States cut off negotiations for cultural exchanges with the Soviet Union after the Afghanistan invasion and again after the Korean airline tragedy—an understandable response to these unprovoked and inexcusable Soviet actions. But it was the wrong response. The need for communication is greater than ever.

I happened to be in the Soviet Union when Frederick Starr, the new president of Oberlin College, arrived with a jazz group he had put together in New Orleans before assuming the Oberlin post. Starr speaks Russian, having taught in the USSR for two years. There were no public announcements of the jazz concerts, but crowds overwhelmed them nonetheless. I mean no disrespect to the New Orleans Repertory Jazz Ensemble when I suggest that the Soviet citizens' response was more than just appreciation of musicianship; they also were expressing their yearning for a reduction of tension.

Why should there not be more exchanges on both sides? Such exchanges are not a substitute for an agreement on nuclear missiles, but they do help to create an atmosphere of understanding, which is essential. *Nations that do not understand each other are not likely to reach accords on arms agreements that will last, if the agreements are reached at all.* Representative Berkley Bedell of Iowa put it another way: "People we get to know usually do not turn out to be those we would like to kill."[23]

Legislators and citizens who are concerned about arms control have to do more than get a nuclear freeze issue on a ballot, or march in a parade, positive as these measures may be.

There is a moral imperative to build a base of understanding, and that is not being done.

☆ 7 ☆

Abortion

That is the heart of this struggle. The quality of life pitted against life. Whichever we choose, we lose.
—Magda Denes

For me personally, that uncertainty on the abortion issue is just enough to tip the scale in favor of the woman who wants an abortion. It is a choice, though, with which I live uneasily. Women have been oppressed through the ages, in great part by being given no choice about their own bodies. As a symbol of a final liberation . . . the right to abortion is powerful.

Yet what a disturbing symbol. For it is a symbol of freedom which can only be realized by crudely affirming still another symbol—the strong killing the weak . . . In killing a fetus, we kill possibility and we kill life.
—Daniel Callahan[2]

The varied reactions to the article about my abortion . . . do not surprise me at all. They are all right. And they are all wrong.
—Linda Bird Francke[3]

I have confronted no issue in the House on which I find myself more torn than abortion. I have not hesitated to take some most unpopular stands on issues about which I believed public opinion in my district wrong. But on abortion both sides are right and both sides are wrong. I envy those who do not struggle within themselves on this issue, who see the moral options as so clear-cut that they can summarize the "truth" about abortion on a bumper-sticker.

/73

I cannot join those who are so prochoice that they see no qualitative difference between a person having an abortion and having an appendectomy. I start from a premise unacceptable to many: that government not only has the obligation to encourage health and opportunities for infants who are born, but also an obligation in some acceptable way to discourage the taking of life before birth.

At the same time, I cannot accept the inflexibility of a Human Life Amendment, as advocated by Right-to-Life proponents. It fails to take into consideration the complex situations in which women find themselves, and it would write into the Constitution standards of behavior the American public is unwilling to accept. It would enter the thicket where religious groups in the United States are deeply committed and deeply divided. Does a woman have no decision whatsoever about the life within her, no matter what conditions brought that life about, no matter what circumstances she faces? Since the time of Moses, wise governments have recognized that there is a difference between a personal moral code and what the law demands, that the law must reflect public opinion or the law is brought into disrepute. Solon, one of the wisest of the leaders of ancient Athens, when asked if he had given the Athenians the best laws possible, replied, "No, but the best they could receive."[4] He recognized the principle that the law must have public support, or it will become void, or worse.

On the other hand, the law can lead public opinion, as it did in school desegregation. But does that comparison apply to the abortion question? Is this decision so personal that the leadership of the law will have little impact?

Men frequently have not been sensitive to the childbearing problems a woman faces, yet men make up the huge majority of federal and state law-making bodies. Martin Luther, who combined greatness and crudeness, wrote: "If a woman grows weary and at last dies from childbearing, it matters not. Let her only die from bearing, she's in there to do it."[5] A man once told me, "Having a baby is no worse than getting a haircut. It's just something women hold over us."

Most societies throughout history have condemned abortion. The ancient Assyrian Code (about 2,000 B.C.) stated: "If a woman of her own accord drops that which is in her, they shall crucify her and not bury her."[6] The Bible mentions abortion only once: "If in a quarrel between men a pregnant woman is hit, so that she miscarries, but is not otherwise injured, the offender shall be fined by the woman's husband with consent of the judges."[7]

The early American attempts to pass laws controlling the practice of abortion were pushed by the medical profession, with neither the secular nor religious press showing much interest. The first U.S. law to mention abortion passed in Connecticut in 1821; the first law about abortion alone passed in Massachusetts in 1845. The post–Civil War feminist movement opposed abortion. In 1867 a Congregational journal condemned abortion as "fashionable murder."[8] In 1869 Roman Catholic Bishop Martin Spalding of Baltimore released a condemnation of abortion on behalf of the Council of Bishops: "No mother is allowed, under any circumstances, to permit the death of her unborn infant, not even for the sake of preserving her own life."[9]

There are a few points on which both sides of the abortion issue agree:

- Two-thirds of the women in the United States who receive abortions are single.
- One-third of the abortions are obtained by women under the age of twenty.
- Abortions are much easier to get in urban areas than in rural areas.
- Abortion is the most common surgical procedure in the United States and in most countries.
- The number of abortions was increasing prior to 1973, but since the 1973 Supreme Court decision on abortion the number of legal abortions more than doubled. The number of deaths of women caused by abortion has dropped, though this figure does not come close to matching the increase in abortions.

The immediate issue that faces Congress each year is a proposal offered by Representative Henry Hyde of Illinois. He regularly introduces an amendment to the appropriations bill that would prohibit the federal government from paying for any abortion to a welfare recipient unless the life of the mother is threatened. The House traditionally accepts his amendment, but the Senate does not. A compromise is worked out that includes cases of incest or rape promptly reported to authorities. An earlier version also allowed for cases where two physicians certified that continued pregnancy would cause severe and long-lasting physical damage to the health of the mother.

No issue Congress faces has the religious community so deeply and so emotionally divided. Most Protestant groups oppose the Hyde amendment because the net effect is that anyone in our society can have an abortion except someone who is poor. Spokespersons for the Roman Catholics, Missouri Synod Lutherans, the Moral Majority, and others say that the idea of the federal government using tax money to pay for abortions is repugnant to the large majority of Americans. Both assumptions are correct.

I have supported broadening the Hyde amendment to permit federal payments for abortion in cases of incest and rape, thereby incurring the wrath of the Right-to-Life people, who list me as being proabortion. Providing federal assistance only for the threatened life of the mother and for incest or rape has meant a decline in federal aid on abortions from approximately 477,000 to 2,000, but there is a serious question whether this change has resulted in any fewer actual abortions taking place. There is some evidence that the result has only been more unsafe abortions.

In 1980 the U.S. Supreme Court ruled that Congress had the right to withhold funding under the Hyde amendment. The court said: "Although government may not place obstacles in the path of a woman's exercise of her freedom of choice, it need not remove those not of its own creation. Indigency falls in that latter category."[10] The dissenting justices commented: "The Hyde amendment is a transparent attempt by the Legislative Branch to impose the political majority's judgment of the morally acceptable and socially desirable preference on a sensitive and intimate decision that the Constitution entrusts to the individual." The Court decision and the Hyde amendment do not stop states from funding abortions for welfare mothers on their own, and fourteen states plus the District of Columbia do that. Those jurisdictions represent 44 percent of the nation's population. It is a significant indication of the deep religious division on the issue that the Roman Catholic bishops sided with the Hyde amendment before the Court, while two of the people who brought the matter to the Supreme Court were officers of the Women's Division of the Board of Global Ministries of the United Methodist Church. The Women's Division itself was one of the appellees. The official position of the United Methodist Church is similar to other mainline Protestant groups: "We believe that continuance of a pregnancy which endangers the life or health of the mother, or poses other serious problems concerning the life, health or mental capability of the child to be, is not a moral necessity. In such a case, we believe the path of mature Christian judgment may indicate the advisability of abortion."[11]

Even more controversial than the Hyde amendment is the Human Life Amendment, a proposal to amend the federal constitution. On this matter I have no struggle in finding an answer, for such an amendment would cause great difficulties, and there is a serious question as to whether it would reduce abortions. The proposal would ban all abortions, making them a federal crime, unless the life of the mother is in peril. There are at least four flaws to the proposal from the perspective of sound public policy:

1. It would make criminals of those who use the intrauterine device (IUD) as a contraceptive. Although I find abortion generally offensive, the microscopic life affected when the IUD is used is so close to nonexistent that use of the IUD does not offend me. Perhaps that is an inconsistency on my part, but it is an inconsistency that many Americans share. Such a law would have the support of only a small percentage of the public. I cannot support a constitutional amendment that calls for criminal indictment of a substantial portion of the population because of the birth control device they use.

2. Abortion because of rape or incest would be a criminal act. Washington journalist Tom Braden's daughter was gang-raped after a Fourth of July fireworks display in the capital city, and she became pregnant. Braden, his wife, and his daughter decided that an abortion was the sensible answer. You and I may agree or disagree with that decision, but most Americans would not want to call the Bradens criminals for making that difficult choice.

3. There are a host of other situations that a rigid constitutional

amendment cannot treat individually. A man in the armed services wrote to me about his wife, pregnant with a child who had neither a spine nor skull. They were told the child would not live more than twenty-four hours if it were born alive. Would he and his wife be criminals if she had an abortion? Under the Human Life Amendment they would.

4. Proponents of this amendment assume that a change in the law would greatly reduce the number of abortions; they also assume that anyone who does not support it is proabortion. It is the same logic that the Prohibitionists used when they said that if you did not favor the Prohibition amendment to the Constitution you were in favor of drunken driving and all the deaths it causes. At the turn of the century twenty-six states petitioned for a convention to amend the Constitution to outlaw polygamy. Did failure to support that mean that a person favored polygamy? How much detail should a constitution carry? For those who like simple, easy, spelled-out answers, the Human Life Amendment is almost perfect because it is unlikely ever to be enacted, and those who support it can maintain their purity of soul and purpose unsullied by reality. It is much simpler than doing something that might be effective.

A study of abortion in various countries suggests that the culture has a great deal more to do with the numbers of abortions than the law. In England, Scotland, and Wales the rates of abortion were much lower than in the United States, prior to the 1973 *Roe* v. *Wade* Supreme Court decision, and yet the laws in the United States were much stricter on abortion.

What can be done to effectively reduce the numbers of abortions?

1. What is clear as other countries are studied is that sex education clearly causes a dramatic drop in abortion rates. There is reluctance in many communities to have the public schools offer sex education courses, for unquestionably moral judgments are made by a teacher in the process. And if there is a decision to make no moral judgments, that in itself is a moral judgment. But what is to prevent some of the churches and synagogues—on both sides of this issue—from teaching sex education? This could even be worked out on a released-time basis with the local public schools, with no one required to take the hours allotted,

and parental permission required. That is more difficult than picketing and parading, and perhaps less emotionally satisfying, but much more effective.

2. Those who oppose abortion can volunteer their homes for young women facing a pregnancy. Many want to keep the knowledge of a pregnancy from people in their immediate community. Providing a temporary home some distance from the home of the mother-to-be provides an alternative that many would welcome.

3. Assistance can be given to groups like Planned Parenthood which have programs that explain birth control options to women and assist them when they want to avoid a pregnancy.

4. Abortions are much more common in other nations than in the United States, particularly developing countries. Part of U.S. foreign aid can be population control programs that explain to the women of these countries how to prevent pregnancy. Some of these programs have resulted in dramatic reductions in both birth rates and abortions.

5. For those who believe that no modification of the 1973 Supreme Court ruling is possible, but that a constitutional amendment is needed, the amendment offered by Senators Orrin Hatch of Utah and Thomas Eagleton of Missouri, remanding this issue to the states, makes much more sense than the Human Life Amendment. The Hatch-Eagleton approach in essence is what we did with Prohibition, permitting each state and, in many instances each community, to decide for itself what the course of action should be. We handle almost all criminal matters at the state and local levels rather than the federal level. The U.S. Constitution outlaws neither murder nor burglary, for example. The weakness of this proposal is that those with money simply go to another state, as they did for liquor following the national repeal of Prohibition. The poor would not have that option. I do not favor this proposal for a constitutional amendment for other reasons as well, but it would not cause the national mischief that the Human Life Amendment would create.

I am troubled by the inconsistencies I see in many of the advocates on both sides. I understand the position of civil-liberties groups in support of the mother-to-be, but too often I detect little interest in or support for the funding of agencies that could prevent unwanted pregnancies, and virtually no interest in assisting women who because of conscience want to avoid an abortion and give birth to a child.

Similarly, I respect such groups as the Roman Catholic bishops, who speak out on abortion as well as on the arms race and the problems facing the poor (as does a marvelous priest, Father James Genesio, in my home town of Carbondale), but I am repelled by those Right-to-Lifers who are noticeably silent on what happens to people after they are born, who show not the slightest concern about massive and severe malnutrition overseas, who support a nuclear buildup as they proclaim their allegiance to the sanctity of life—whose focus is so narrow that it offends the large majority of members of Congress. The Moral Majority and their spokesmen wax eloquent about "baby killing," but never support programs that help the emotional and physical health of mothers, never speak out in behalf of poor families who face severe economic problems with unwanted children, and never raise a whisper about babies starving in Africa, or those who are neglected at home.

I do not see any national consensus emerging on the abortion issue. The nation must struggle with it, and for many of us that means that an internal as well as a political struggle must continue. The path of my struggle is littered with inconsistencies in voting pattern; I suppose that is the pattern of internal struggles. I have gradually moved to the point where I believe this issue is so fraught with deep personal and religious experiences and attitudes that it is not the role of government to impose answers. Whenever people start from a moral and religious base and reach precisely opposite conclusions, then government ordinarily should not attempt to dictate answers. There is also a serious question in my mind whether federal government attempts to dictate answers would result in anything constructive, for apparently among the nations with the highest rates of abortion are those that totally outlaw abortions.

As Linda Bird Franke writes: "There are no neat answers to the question of abortion, and perhaps there never will be."[12]

☆ **8** ☆

Religion

Among politicians the esteem of religion is profitable; the principles of it are troublesome.
—Benjamin Whichcote, 1753[1]

Those who see in politics one of the most cynical manifestations of sin and refuse to be mixed up with it, actually end up much against their will supporting the most scandalous forms of it.
—Phillipe Maury[2]

A nation must have a religion, and that religion must be under the control of the government.
—Napoleon, 1801[3]

The first debate to which I listened in the House of Lords was . . . during World War II. There was a solemn argument as to whether contraceptives should be issued to British troops. For hours the lay peers discussed the morality of the question until, at last, the Bishop of St. Alban's rose in his white lawn sleeves to speak for the Lords Spiritual, the bench of bishops. It was not for him, he said, speaking for the church, to enter into the questions of morality that were involved; those could be left safely to the Lords Temporal. But with the fall of Singapore, the rubber supplies of the Empire had been seriously endangered. . . .Rubber was urgently needed for the tires of aircraft wheels; should it be wasted on contraceptives? "Hear, hear!" murmured the Lords Temporal, most of whom had been absolute bounders when they were junior officers;

and as I left the Palace of Westminster, I found myself hum-
ming, "There'll Always Be an England."

—Henry Fairlie[4]

Political religion and religious politics are sometimes highly
visible on the congressional scene, and that which is the most
visible tends also to be the most superficial. Political reporter
Henry Fairlie has noted: "There is always a tendency for the
name of God, when it is let loose in the political arena, to get
out of control."[5] There is another side that is less visible and of
greater depth. No one can measure it, but it is there. The religious dimension in Congress and the nation shows itself in ways
that sometimes embarrass us and sometimes make us proud. An
indication that religion plays a strong role in the cultural life of
the country is that almost as many people attend church on a
single Sunday as go to the nation's major sporting events during
the whole year. In Congress there is both the superficial and the
substantial; Congress reflects the nation.

I enter a discussion of religion with one warning: I claim
neither great knowledge, nor to be one of the better practitioners.
Having grown up in a Lutheran parsonage I have some sensitivities to the world of religion. But I feel a little like the de-
fendant in a story lawyers tell, who received a sentence of 145
years. "Your honor, I'm forty-five years old," the prisoner pleaded,
"there is no way I can serve out the sentence." The judge leaned
forward and gently said, "Do the best you can." I don't even
claim to be doing the best I can. When I am accosted on the
street by a stranger who asks, "Are you a Christian?" I can only
reply, "Yes, but an inadequate one."

One of the finest persons in terms of nobility of character ever
to serve in the House is Jerry Voorhis, who was defeated for
reelection by a young Navy veteran named Richard Nixon. Asked
to comment on his role as a Christian politician, Voorhis responded, "I cannot say that I was a Christian politician. I can
say that I tried to be."[6]

Members of Congress, no less than others, want to find meaning in life. Historian Will Durant has written: "Science gives man
ever greater powers but less significance; it improves his tools
but neglects his purposes . . . it gives life and history no meaning

or worth that is not canceled by death or omnivorous time."[7] All of us recognize the truth of that. Members are on a fast track, dealing one moment with a bill to declare National Pickle Week and the next with an issue that bears on the frightening arms race. For many members religious moorings, often totally separate from any organized church, as was the case with Abraham Lincoln, are significant. There is probably less respect for the details of dogma among members than you might find in the general public, but more of an awareness of the vastness of humanity and the universe, and more general acceptance of assumptions about the meaning of it all, though there are those who "believe in nothing higher than the roofs of their houses," as Saint Bernardino said in the fifteenth century.

There is the internal religious life, the use and abuse of religion by office holders and candidates, and the use and abuse of politics by those who are religious leaders.

One summer between my senior year in high school and my freshman year in college I worked as a substitute mail carrier. One cloudless day as I walked between two homes I spotted a beautiful gray cat suddenly grab a robin and hold it securely in its jaws. The robin protested with desperate sounds I had never heard from a bird. I chased the cat for a moment or two, hoping to save the robin, and then stood by helplessly while the cat tore the robin apart and ate it. A beautiful cat and a beautiful robin. The scene is as clear to me now as when it happened thirty-eight years ago. It taught me something about life, and it introduced me to a phenomenon no one has ever explained adequately: the presence of evil. I have seen it in its extreme forms: child abuse and the terrorizing of innocent people by underworld figures. It is also evident in a host of less dramatic, more common ways. I do not understand the evil in myself, or in others, or in life given to all creatures by the force greater than ourselves we call God.

Legislators, who see more of the joy and tragedy of life than most people, have to recognize the existence of evil in all of us, as well as the good. We struggle with how we balance these forces within ourselves, within the nation, and within the laws that we enact.

We have a House and a Senate chaplain and the two of them provide personal assistance to members and the staff, often meaningful assistance. There are times when people under constant pressure need someone to talk to, someone from whom they can receive counsel. The chaplaincy, now under attack in the courts for its constitutionality, offers an important but little-noticed service.

There are organized ways we approach our inner struggles, the "prayer breakfast" perhaps being the most noteworthy. In fact, this is a misnomer; it does not at all resemble the mammoth publicly attended President's Prayer Breakfasts or the Governor's Prayer Breakfasts, which strike me as being long on display and short on religion. The weekly House breakfast (Senators also have one) is limited to members—no reporters, no spouses, no staff. Each week a member talks about his or her philosophy of life, what problems we face. Discussion usually follows. There are about thirty members at the average breakfast. Some of the presentations are thoughtful and some totally lacking in depth. There is no orthodoxy about the presentations, though there is at times a lack of sensitivity to the Jewish member or two who sometimes comes. What is said remains with us. I recall the time a member (no longer in the House) said, "I'm not sure I believe in God," and then told of his religious search. The opposition party members present could easily have leaked it to the press, but no one did. I do not suggest that those who attend these breakfasts are any more religious or in any sense better than the other members, but I appreciate the meetings and frequently get more from them than I do from a Sunday service. There is in the group, I believe, a general awareness of the validity of Reinhold Niebuhr's statement, "Most of the evil in this world does not come from evil people. It comes from people who consider themselves good."[8]

There has been one quasi-scientific study of religion and Congress, *Religion on Capitol Hill: Myths and Realities* by Peter L. Benson and Dorothy L. Williams. They write that for 24 percent of the members religion is a major influence on their voting; for 56 percent, a moderate influence; for 19 percent, a minor influence; and for 1 percent, no influence. Self-analysis is always suspect, and particularly self-analysis that we report to others, so I question these figures. But I do not question the authors' conclusion: "Religion is powerfully related to behavior."[9]

Religion sometimes is abused by members and office seekers. Candidates and officials too often try to wrap their political beliefs in the cloak of religion, in an artificial piousness that discredits both politics and religion. Speaking of such an official, Tom Wicker wrote: "His gift is that he can touch his shabby cause with a peculiar moral gloss. With unerring instinct he can arouse latent racial antagonism while appealing to common sense and Christian duty."[10]

Few candidates suggest that they belong to no church. Affiliation is almost a requirement, but membership is often little more than on paper, an affiliation that is likely to be mentioned in campaign literature. If an area is heavily Catholic or Lutheran or Baptist or Jewish, and the candidate is of that affiliation, the campaign literature will make sure to mention it, sometimes in a low-key way. What is proper and what is improper is not always easy to determine. Before an election there usually are special invitations to visit certain churches in my district, sometimes with an invitation to speak. A year before an election I am pleased to accept; four weeks before an election I feel uneasy and usually decline, unless it is an occasion such as that offered by Calvary Baptist Church of Marion, Illinois, which invites all candidates to say a word or two. There is no question that the religiosity of politicians tends to increase as an election approaches.

It is easy to look back into history and see the misuse and errors of the application of religion to politics, much more difficult to accurately assess current happenings. The use of religion and the symbol of the cross by the Ku Klux Klan is an obvious example of such abuse.

The tyranny of Hitler became possible in large measure because Christian leaders failed to speak up for the Jews and in opposition to evils perpetrated by the Nazis. The religious leaders—largely Catholic and Lutheran—decided to "stay out of politics." There were a few exceptions such as Dietrich Bonnhoeffer, but embarrassingly few. Church leadership purchased temporary comfort and immunity through neutrality, but at the cost of troubled consciences and ultimately massive bloodshed. They felt that if they kept their personal purity they would remain untainted by the state.

The Catholic and Lutheran leaders of Germany were not alone. The same confusion of personal and public morality made by some television preachers today also afflicted many U.S. church leaders during the Hitler period. Baptists are easy to pinpoint because they held a Baptist World Alliance congress in Berlin in 1934. The *Official Report of the Fifth Baptist World Congress* notes: "Chancellor Adolf Hitler gives . . . the prestige of his personal example since he neither uses intoxicants nor smokes."[11] The president of the Southern Baptist Theological Seminary in Louisville cautioned "against too-hasty judgment of a leader who has stopped German women from smoking cigarettes and wearing red lipstick in public."[12] A Boston pastor-delegate wrote: "It was a great relief to be in a country where salacious sex literature cannot be sold. . . . The new Germany has burned great masses of corrupting books and magazines along with its bonfires of Jewish and communistic libraries."[13] The racism of Hitler did not bother many of the Southern Baptists who were defending racism back home. And they saw in Hitler a stop to communism. A Montgomery, Alabama, delegate commented that Nazism "is for Germany a safe step in the right direction. Nazism has at least been a bar to . . . Bolshevism."[14] Baptists were far from alone, unfortunately. For example, Frank Buchman, leader of the Moral Re-Armament group wrote: "I thank heaven for a man like Adolph Hitler, who built a front-line defense against the anti-Christ of communism."[15]

President Reagan's speech to the National Association of Evangelicals, in which he called the U.S.–Soviet arms race a "struggle between right and wrong and good and evil,"[16] is another example of the same mistake, of leaping to huge conclusions about the presence of good and evil. It offers a stark contrast to Abraham Lincoln's less popular but more realistic second inaugural address in which he recognized good and evil on both sides. In the midst of a nation torn by a bitterness we had never known and have not known since, Lincoln said:

> Neither party expected for the war the magnitude or the duration which it has already attained. . . . Both read the same

Bible, and pray to the same God; and each invokes his aid against the other. . . . Let us judge not, that we be not judged. . . . With malice toward none; with charity for all; with firmness in the right, as God gives us to see the right, let us strive on to finish the work we are in . . . to do all which may achieve and cherish a just and lasting peace among ourselves, and with all nations.

A hasty jump from personal morality to public morality can be dangerous, whether in Berlin or Washington, D.C. Equally clear is that opposition to one form of public immorality, as most of us in the United States conceive communism, should not cause an automatic embrace of whatever or whoever opposes that immorality. What is true of one public immorality is true of others. Oppose what is wrong, but do not immediately accept any idea or person who opposes that wrong.

Religion shows up in congressional halls in very organized ways, sometimes good, sometimes bad. There are times when I believe the nation's political leadership is more religious than the nation's religious leadership, and the nation's religious leadership is more political than the nation's political leadership.

For example, in political life we seem to understand the doctrine of sin more fully than many theologians do. I can be in a vigorous debate with an adversary on the floor of the House, and then have lunch with that person. Both of us are completely sincere in the positions we take, but we have developed the ability to "disagree without being disagreeable"; to recognize that those who oppose us are just as sincere as we are; and to understand there is always the possibility, however remote, that we just might be wrong. Theologians, who write volumes about the innate sinfulness of man, often are much less able to recognize the possibility of error in themselves. They may denounce the doctrine of papal infallibility, but not their own. So church disputes tend to be more personally bitter than disputes we have on the floor of the House or Senate, though occasionally we have encounters that are just as bitter.

Church and politics mix in a variety of ways, sometimes during an election. In the 1980 election Boston's Cardinal Humberto

Medeiros sent Roman Catholics of that area a strongly worded message on abortion—and on abortion only—that virtually called for the defeat of Representatives James Shannon and Barney Frank. It was heavy-handed, and Catholics responded by helping Shannon and Frank win by overwhelming margins. In 1982 Cardinal Medeiros and four other Massachusetts bishops issued a statement in line with the policy of the National Council of Bishops, urging people to vote, listing many issues that should concern Catholics, including abortion. Editorial writers and Catholic leaders who had criticized the tone of the earlier message applauded this one.

Most who try to apply the tenets of faith to the world of politics do so with the recognition that the application of religious principles to life is a somewhat uncertain business, and there is a possibility of being wrong. But there are some in both the liberal and conservative camps who take rigidly dogmatic stands, and charge that those who disagree are morally inferior. Foremost among these is the Moral Majority, headed by the Reverend Jerry Falwell. One of the Moral Majority's promotional brochures modestly notes that just as God sent forth Adam, Moses, John the Baptist, George Washington, and Abraham Lincoln in difficult times, so too in this troubled period has he sent forth Jerry Falwell.[17] The appeal of a Moral Majority–type operation is threefold:

First, it points to things that are wrong in our society and calls for action. Too much graphic violence on television and in the movies is an example of a complaint on which I can agree with the Moral Majority, though not with their cure. Some of the wrongs these people see are real, some simply the result of changing life-styles, and some exaggerations. An example of exaggeration is a full-page "Open Letter from Jerry Falwell" in the *Washington Post* calling on "the loyal members of Congress" (presumably some of us are disloyal) to oppose the nuclear freeze resolution. The statement notes that the "Soviets have almost a two-to-one advantage in nuclear weapons,"; the reality is that the United States has more nuclear warheads than the Soviets.[18] The advertisement contained so many inaccuracies that it had little impact on Congress, but many unsuspecting readers of the full-page message probably believed it. *Time* magazine said: "The

Moral Majority's wide attraction is a sign that large numbers of Americans are sick of a society in which so many standards of conduct have collapsed."[19]

Second, Moral Majority and its counterparts on the Right and Left speak with an Olympian certainty that is appealing. The public longs for solid, clear-cut answers, right or wrong. The Moral Majority provides answers in which good is good and evil is evil, and there is nothing in between.

The third appeal that a Jerry Falwell has is the advantage of distance, an appeal religious leaders had until recent times. No longer is the parish priest or local minister or rabbi some distant, respected, revered figure but someone much more a part of the community, whose weaknesses and strengths are known. An aura the local clergy once had is missing, while television personalities, whose packaged product enters your living room, remain unblemished figures; their calls for action are not diminished by the knowledge that they have a short temper or an overdraft at the local bank or they spend too much time playing golf. There is a tendency to place more faith in the assertions of a distant figure than the person who drinks a cup of coffee with you in the local restaurant.

The *Christian Voice* publishes ratings based on the Moral Majority stands. The first year of *Christian Voice* ratings I received zero out of a possible 100 percent. Former Representative Robert Drinan, a Roman Catholic priest, also received zero; Representative Robert Edgar, a Methodist minister, managed 8 percent; and one of our colleagues found guilty in the Abscam scandal, who made national television stuffing twenty-five thousand dollars into his pockets, received a 100-percent rating. In targeted districts (such as mine) the Sunday before the 1982 election a four-page "Congressional Report Card" describing "Key Moral Issues prepared especially for Christians by Christian Voice Moral Government Fund" was distributed on car windshields.[20] In it my opponent was described as believing that "the traditional Christian values must be a part of our government." He was quoted: "I believe in God. I am a Christian that [sic] believes Jesus Christ's death on the cross gave me my opportunity to eternal life in heaven." Without specifically saying that I don't share these values and beliefs, the "report card" noted my votes on the "key moral issues." It stated that I voted against a balanced budget (a blatant inaccuracy), using as evidence a vote on a budget substitute that cut programs for the poor and increased defense spending, an amendment that actually would have increased deficits. I voted against the amendment that would have increased deficits. I voted against the amendment that would have stopped school busing for integration, an equally clear "immoral" vote in their eyes. I opposed the amendment that would have prevented the Internal Revenue Service from taking tax-exempt status away from private schools that racially discriminate. They do not list the vote that way. The brochure says I voted against protecting Christian schools. I am listed as wrong on prayer in the schools. The list goes on. The folder adds this warning from Proverbs 29:2: "When the righteous are in authority, the people rejoice; but when the wicked beareth rule, the people mourn." They were not very subtle in suggesting in which camp I belong. I am sure many were misled by this "report card"; judging by remarks in their sermons, at least a few ministers were.

Among almost all members of Congress, conservatives and liberals alike, the Moral Majority does not get high marks. There is an arrogance about assuming the mantle of morality, implying that those who disagree are immoral. Their literature consistently twists the meaning of votes—not good politics, not good religion, and not moral. This is the same group that does not touch on the subject of world hunger, but says a member of Congress has cast an immoral vote if he or she wishes to slow down the arms race. One of the issues that concerned both the *Christian Voice* and the Moral Majority was appropriations for centers for battered spouses. These are refuges for wives who face physical harm at home. My vote for funding them was listed as an "anti-family" vote. Is part of healthy family life occasionally beating your wife? I can tolerate someone opposing me on that funding issue, though I have difficulty understanding it; but to wrap such a stance in the cloak of morality and religion is an abuse of both.

It is not only ancient Herod who gets tempted with the idea that his is "a voice of a god and not of a man."[21] Representative Jim Wright has written: "Few tyrannies are worse than tyrannical churchmen acting out of a sense of divine, infallible mission."[22]

Even Cromwell appealed to the leaders of the Church of Scotland: "I beseech you, in the bowels of Christ, to think it possible you may be mistaken."[23] Peter Berger, a contemporary writer, comments: "The idea that moral sensitivity somehow bestows the competence to make policy recommendations on every subject is delusional. . . . The consequence has been inflationary prophecy."[24] Lord Acton once described the church as "a gilded crutch of absolutism."[25] In different ways that description contains truth a century later.

Although the television-religion-politics gilded church is mostly a politically conservative phenomenon, liberals are not immune from the same temptations. Those of liberal religious and political persuasion can be equally dogmatic and assertive, though the names under which they operate are less patently offensive than Moral Majority.

An inappropriate injection of religion into politics is not a new American phenomenon. We experienced it in the 1928 and 1960 presidential elections when the Catholicism of Al Smith and John F. Kennedy became the dominant issue. In the last century the Know-Nothings tried to build on religious prejudice. The 1776 Constitution of North Carolina prohibited Roman Catholics, Jews, atheists, and anarchists from holding public office, and it prohibited active clergymen from being in the state legislature. The Delaware charter of 1701 gave the right to hold public office to "all persons who also profess to believe in Jesus Christ, the Saviour of the world."[26] The Maryland Constitution of 1776 granted religious liberty to all "professing the Christian religion."[27] But compared to the European applications of religion to political life, the American experience was tame. The Spanish Inquisition not only executed heretics, it also became an opportunity for office holders to confiscate the wealth of those killed. "Corruption flourished piously," one historian noted.[28] In Europe burning as punishment for witchcraft was common; in the sixteenth century fourteen witches were sent to the stake in Geneva (population then about twenty thousand) for persuading Satan to inflict a plague on that city. Calvin, Luther, Erasmus, Sir Thomas More, and numerous popes all supported punishment for witchcraft. Calvinist Geneva's laws had probably the most details, including the number of dishes permitted at a meal. A father was imprisoned for naming his son Claude instead of Abraham. In one case a child was beheaded for striking his parents. Torture of the most extreme sort was generally accepted throughout Europe. Executions were frequent. Time and distance and a frequently enlightened leadership in what became the United States softened the harsh aspects of the European experience in applying religious principles to civil subjects here.

The use of religion to justify questionable actions is, however, a thread that also runs through U.S. history. Before the outbreak of the Spanish-American War, President William McKinley sent a message to Congress: "If it shall hereafter appear to be a duty imposed by our obligations to ourselves, to civilization and humanity to intervene with force it shall be done without fault on our part and only because the necessity for such action will be so clear as to command the support and the approval of the civilized world. . . . I speak not of forcible annexation for that cannot be thought of. That by our code of morals would be criminal aggression."[29] When the Philippines were annexed he brought God to the rescue: "I am not ashamed to tell you gentlemen that I went on my knees and prayed to Almighty God for light and guidance more than one night. And one night it came to me this way—that there was nothing left for us to do but to take them all, and to educate the Filipinos, and uplift and civilize and Christianize them, and by God's grace do the very best we could do by them, as our fellowmen for whom Christ also died."[30]

The two presidents who spelled out their religious beliefs most clearly were Woodrow Wilson and Jimmy Carter. Both received some criticism from coreligionists for their application of faith to their duties. In the case of Jimmy Carter, for example, two authors in a religious journal suggested to him that the world "is not a gymnasium for the exercise of personal morality."[31] And that "God-talk tends to be used by politicians to mystify social reality."[32] Two other presidents who showed above-average religious reflection but who were much less precise about their beliefs were Thomas Jefferson and Abraham Lincoln. Interestingly, Jefferson, who today would be called a Unitarian, has been quietly annexed as a trinitarian by some who tend to exaggerate the virtues of the nation's founders.

Most who engage in political activity today in the name of

religion conduct themselves responsibly. They take strong positions but readily acknowledge the possibility that they might be wrong. These include the Roman Catholic bishops, almost all the mainline Protestant churches, and groups such as Bread for the World. I do not always agree with the stands the various groups take, but there is an element of tolerance that the glazed-eye types do not have. The approach used by the less dogmatic is both sounder and more effective. It varies from letters and phone calls, to the occasional breakfasts some of us will have with religious leaders. Sometimes resolutions are adopted, messages go out to key church leaders, and action by congregations is advocated. The clearest example of church influence in recent decades came in the great civil rights debates of the 1960s when the churches thrust themselves into a position of strong leadership. Key political leaders such as Senator Everett Dirksen, who had previously opposed civil rights legislation, ended up advocating it, declaring this a moral issue, an attitude the religious leaders had created. When religious leaders take a stand, in some loosely coordinated and united manner, and follow through month after month and year after year, the body politic ultimately will respond. Although the record of organized religion has not been unblemished—far from it—it has, on balance, been a force for good, whether through the creation of hospitals and orphanages, or through supporting the English barons in their revolt against King John and drawing up the Magna Charta. The late, distinguished political scientist Hans J. Morgenthau noted: "Many of the most important modern insights about politics have come from the pens of theologians."[33]

An example of a balanced approach (and I acknowledge some prejudice since I agree with their stand) is the Roman Catholic bishops' statement on nuclear armament. Carefully drawn, with no pretense that all bishops agree with it, nor an assumption that they have a monopoly on the truth, it discusses a major moral issue. The bishops do not imply that those who disagree are any less nobly motivated. The weakness of the process followed by the bishops on this issue is that it took so long to emerge. There is no such luxury of time ordinarily. On most issues religious leaders and lobbyists—and legislators—must make decisions quickly.

To be effective, to be true to its traditions, organized religion must enter the realm of the controversial. Religious historian Martin Marty said: "An inoffensive church is a contradiction in terms."[34]

After I spoke to an assembly at Morningside College in Iowa, two faculty members, Douglas and Rita Swan, both Ph.D.s, came to me with a problem that illustrates the complexity of the religiously related decisions Congress must make. The Swans were Christian Scientists until recently. Their sixteen-month-old child became seriously ill and they used the services of a Christian Science healer, instead of medical help. Their child died. They are convinced that had the government not recognized their right to practice their religion in the case of a seriously ill child they would not have suffered this crushing loss. They charge that current regulations of the Department of Health and Human Services result in "religiously influenced medical neglect of children."[35] The Glory Barn Church in Indiana, now known as the Faith Assembly, has only 1,760 members nationwide, "yet ten newborns or their mothers belonging to that church died without medical attention between 1976 and 1980."[36] An Indiana newspaper reports that the number "of medical-neglect deaths linked to the six-year-old church [is] at least twenty-six."[37] In Philadelphia five children in one family who belonged to a similar small group died of pneumonia without medical attention. Our attitude in Congress has been to go out of our way to respect the religious beliefs of citizens, and that should continue. But where do we draw the line? Anyone who believes the issue is easily resolved has not studied the problem, has not talked with people like the Swans, or has come to the discussion with dogmatic presumptions of right and wrong.

There are many issues on which decisions must be made along church-state lines. Should there be tuition tax credit for nonpublic schools? Should school lunch funds be available for nonpublic schools? Should the House and Senate and the armed forces have chaplains? Should the Postal Service issue stamps honoring Saint Francis of Assisi and Martin Luther? Should evolution be taught in the public schools? The questions are almost endless. Religious commentator James Wall provides another example: "When Jerry Ford pardoned Richard Nixon for all crimes committed in office, he made it a point to let us know that he attended church on the day of the decision and then prayed about it. What are we to conclude? Either that God told Ford to grant the pardon, or that Ford was a shrewd politician who thought it would be smart to provide his actions with a religious cover, or a combination of the two."[38]

Groups such as Americans United for Separation of Church and State espouse Jefferson's belief, noted in a letter to a Baptist association, that there should be "a wall of separation" between church and state. Although I differ with this group on many of their stands, they perform an important public service in raising questions of propriety and constitutionality. Others, at the opposite end of the spectrum, sense no problems and would have the church financially supported by the state to a much greater extent. Somewhere there is a proper balance. The Constitution did not mandate a separation, but that there would be no established state church. I have no problem with federal assistance on a welfare basis, provided the same assistance is available to all others. If the local Methodist church is on fire, for example, I favor calling out the fire department. If someone says, "Separation of church and state; we can't do it," he or she is following the "wall of separation" theory, but as long as the fire protection is available to all groups, there is no harm in sending the fire department to assist, and a positive good to the community results. The same principles apply in other situations.

On the other hand, the Supreme Court decision that says no government can prescribe a prayer for those in public schools seems to me an eminently sound decision that in no way attacks religious beliefs, in fact protects them. I do not favor a constitutional amendment to negate that decision. Citizens should not expect the schools to do what homes and churches and synagogues should do. There is *some* truth to Walter Lippmann's statement about our culture: "We have succeeded in substituting trivial illusions for majestic faiths."[39] But great caution must be exercised as to what the role of government should be even if you agree with Lippmann's conclusion.

The church-state struggles in areas where the two interests obviously mesh or collide is only a small part of the religion and politics question. How should the religious leaders influence the host of governmental decisions that have moral implications? How should those of us who serve in the political arena practice religion without abusing it? Where does the blending of personal religious belief and political belief take us? A French writer says that the "greatest danger that threatens the church in carrying out its political ministry is the temptation of taking itself too seriously."[40] There is an element of truth to that, a truth that keeps sensitive religious leaders from the temptation of absolutism. But how can you be properly serious and effective, yet not pompous and pious? How can flawed humanity strive for the good and just, at the same time recognizing the flaws? Will the religious people who think themselves good and virtuous be willing to soil themselves in the earthy world of politics?

Poet Chad Walsh has written:

Forgive us our virtues,
As we forgive those who are virtuous against us.[41]

☆ 9 ☆

The Political Parties

I always voted at my party's call,
And I never thought of thinking for myself at all.
—*H.M.S. Pinafore*[1]

Those who think that all virtue is to be found in their own
party principles push matters to extremes; they do not consider that disproportion destroys a state. . . . The legislator
and the statesmen ought to know what democratic measures
save and what destroy.
—Aristotle[2]

JOHNSON: They who are governed by absolute princes are
governed by chance. There is no security for good government.
CAMBRIDGE: There have been many sad victims to absolute
government.
JOHNSON: So, sir, have there been to popular factions.
BOSWELL: The question is, which is worse, one wild beast or
many?
—James Boswell, *Life of Johnson*, 1791[3]

A host of political observers agree that the two political parties in the United States must be strengthened, but George
Kennan tells us that the two parties "cater to what is basest in
the American electorate," hardly an endorsement for increased
responsibility.[4] Our two political parties are an accident of history, though from the earliest times the divisions have existed
that separated Alexander Hamilton and Thomas Jefferson: vot-

ing only by property owners as opposed to the broader franchise. In 1513 Niccolò Machiavelli wrote:

> A principality is created either by the people or by the nobles, accordingly as one or other of them has the opportunity; for the nobles, seeing they cannot withstand the people, begin to cry up the reputation of one of themselves, and they make him a prince so that under his shadow they can give vent to their ambitions. The people, finding they cannot resist the nobles, also cry up the reputation of one of themselves, and make him a prince so as to be defended by his authority.[5]

Those two divisions, changing the name "nobles" to "propertied class" or "big business" or whatever category you prefer, have existed down through the centuries. Motivation is generally not as consciously self-serving as Machiavelli suggests, but the two basic divisions remain today. Although in general it is easy to see where today's U.S. political parties stand, there are many within each party who fit more comfortably philosophically into the other camp, and historically there have been a few times when party leadership traded roles. What should the attitude of a responsible legislator be to his or her political party? There are two thrusts and they are in conflict. The first is the recognition that the two major political parties within the United States ought to be strengthened, and the second is that people of conscience cannot be too tightly bound to a party position.

Most Americans agree that the two-party political system has served us well. In the academic community there are some who disagree, arguing that the two parties are so generalized they do not give people the chance to express their viewpoints in a focused way. This book is not the place to engage in that debate. The fact is that we are now dealing with a two-party system and are likely to be doing so for decades to come. The accidents of history that brought us the two-party system, enshrined in practice more than statute, have been fortunate, for the two-party system has been an effective agent of progress, getting people to support causes they might not otherwise support, and a unifying force within the country, pulling toward the center and rejecting extreme positions. The two-party system is an agent for self-restraint.

The two political groups—which tend to be local and state parties rather than national—perform with reasonable skill the function of helping people get elected. But from the viewpoint of issue and governance, the two-party system does not look as good. I doubt that there are five members of the House and Senate who have read the political platform of either national party from the last presidential election—and I am among the nonreaders, for those of us in Congress know there are few documents with less meaning than a party platform. It is an appeal for votes that surfaces in a presidential election year, but once the candidate is selected, neither the presidential nominee nor the party's other candidates pay more than passing attention to the platform.

Party responsibility for governance is also flawed. The leaders whom House and Senate members select are often leaders in name more than substance. The Speaker of the House, for example, cannot remove a member from a committee and has virtually no power over the actions of a member. The result is government that too often tends toward the chaotic, with 435 House members going in as many directions; the 100 senators do the same. Almost a century ago someone said that the House of Representatives is "a scuffle of local interests in which every member must take his part under penalty of losing his seat. 'What has he done for his district?' is a question which applies the test by which ordinarily the value of a representative is gauged."[6] That results in scattered responsibility. In 1983 political observer Theodore White noted: "How does a nation live with a Congress that counts more brilliant men than ever before but cannot lead, and will follow no leadership?"[7] Even when the president of the United States works out some compromise with the spokesmen for the two parties in Congress, there is no assurance the leaders can deliver. The public likes that, although not perhaps in each and every instance. Early in this century an observer spoke for many: "I cannot trust a party; I can trust a man. I cannot hold a party responsible; I can hold a man responsible. I cannot get an expression of opinion which is single and simple from a party;

I can get that only from a man."[8] So our politics has tended toward personalities more than party or issue.

In the last two decades straight party voting has declined and single-issue orientations have become more prominent. The overall public attention to issues is no more focused; certainly there is no more party responsibility for issues. We continue to spread responsibility among each and every member of Congress rather than within a party, and the members vote as they please. Political scientist Austin Ranney came uncomfortably close to the truth when he said: "In the American system . . . the parties consider winning power to be their sole end. When power is won, their job is completed."[9]

Parliamentary systems have the opposite weakness: members have to go along or the government falls. There is limited room for differences of opinion within a party. This is true of a few state and local legislative bodies also. When I first served in the Illinois General Assembly, party discipline was severe, enforced by a patronage system that gave power to a few who controlled the jobs. In Congress if you vote with your party leadership three-fourths of the time you are considered a fairly down-the-line party person; but in the Illinois General Assembly when I differed 5 percent of the time with the party leadership, centralized at the time in the mayor of Chicago, the media described me as a maverick. Party discipline remains greater in the Illinois legislature than in most state bodies, but court decisions on job appointments and various reforms have diminished the awesome power patronage once enforced. At one time Lyndon Johnson could call on Richard Daley to deliver Illinois votes in Congress, and Franklin D. Roosevelt could call on Frank Hague of New Jersey. Local leaders (and they were always local) of political parties—called "bosses" by their opponents—helped to provide a sense of party discipline. The party power brokers have been replaced by the money brokers and party discipline is further diluted. When Ronald Reagan needs votes, he calls the large contributors to get at the members.

Thoughtful observers, such as newsman David Broder and academicians from Woodrow Wilson to Jack Peltason, have urged greater responsibility for governance. Twenty-eight years before he became president, Wilson wrote: "The more power is divided, the more irresponsible it becomes."[10] A few years later, in 1893, Wilson sounded a note that might have been written today: "The grave social and economic problems that now thrust themselves forward . . . indicate that our system is already aging, and that any clumsiness, looseness, or irresponsibility in government action must prove a source of grave and increasing peril. . . . Instead of the present arrangements for compromise, piecemeal legislation, we must have coherent plans from recognized party leaders and means for holding those leaders to a faithful execution of their plans in clear-cut Acts of Congress."[11] Greater party responsibility is needed, Wilson stressed repeatedly. There is a need, but with greater power to the party will go increasing problems for the legislator of conscience. How far do you go in turning over your vote to partisan leaders? What is the responsibility of the legislator to his or her political group?

The issue of party responsibility emerges occasionally in Democratic caucuses. Twice in my nine years in the House we have had extensive discussions about party responsibility. The most lengthy took place in an executive session of the caucus on September 16, 1981, after President Reagan had won several battles on his budget and tax programs because a substantial number of Democrats voted with him. It became a matter of concern because the majority of Democrats opposed the proposals, and because many of those who crossed over and voted with the president said privately they thought the programs were bad. But pressures from their districts, or from their contributors, or sweet talk and promises from the president, or a combination of all factors got them to support the Reagan proposals.

The caucus chairman, Representative Gillis Long of Louisiana, brought the matter before the Democrats because, he said, many thought "that steps should be taken to discipline those members who defected."[12] He felt the matter should be brought to the caucus for discussion and said he wanted to focus the discussion on what the "reasonable bounds of political conduct [are] for a member who receives benefits from his political party."[13] Until 1975 a two-thirds vote of the caucus in theory could bind the votes of Democratic members. This "King Caucus" rule came as part of a move to lessen the power of Speaker Joe Cannon in the early 1900s. Democrats used the rule six times between 1911 and 1924, and twice between 1925 and 1975, when the caucus dropped the rule. In 1965 and again in 1969 the caucus voted to strip members of committee seniority for supporting the Republican presidential candidates; that rule probably would be imposed again by Democrats if there were a repetition of the 1981 Reagan budget/tax votes. In 1983 the Steering and Policy Committee of the Democratic caucus voted to drop Representative Phil Gramm of Texas, who had been leading budgetary efforts for the Republicans, as a Democratic member of the powerful Budget Committee. The Democratic caucus approved that action. Gramm resigned from the House and was reelected as a Republican in a special election.

The 1981 caucus grew out of a feeling that a few Democrats were abusing privileges by attending Democratic caucuses, then going down to the White House for meetings with Republican leaders. "You can't be in the huddles of both teams," was a refrain heard many times. Representative Toby Moffett of Connecticut also complained that those few were "absolutely rubbing the noses of the rest of us in the mud [being] seen on national television every second or third day, standing smilingly behind the President of the United States."[14]

As a vehicle for discussion Representative Long used a resolution praising the Democratic party and calling on the caucus "to develop and promote policies designed to meet the challenges of the 1980s."[15] Representative Jim Mattox of Texas (now attorney general of that state) called the resolution "hogwash."[16] Representative Charles Rangel of New York commented: "Let me compliment you on this resolution, Mr. Chairman, which says absolutely nothing, but I think it is therapeutic. . . . It does give us an opportunity to get together and talk about our frustrations."[17] Rangel added that out of loyalty to the party he had "paid his dues" on issues, while others were trying to take advantage of the party without paying their dues. Representative Thomas Downey of New York urged that the opportunity to serve on the most powerful committees be reserved for those reasonably faithful to the party.

To vote with the opposition party at the time of organizing the House or Senate would clearly be considered a violation of party responsibility. To be in the caucus of one party and then plan strategy with the other also is irritating to colleagues. To be too public about working with the other side on a major controversial issue is a lesser offense, but does not endear a member to his or her fellow party members. However, voting your convictions—if they are really your convictions—is not something I hear criticized often. For example, Representative Charles Bennett of Florida votes more conservatively than most Democratic members, but everyone understands these are his deep-felt convictions; I have never heard him criticized for that voting pattern.

Leaders of both parties do come and "bend your arm" to go along. A former member has written: "Convinced Christians will seldom be able to be absolutely 'regular' in their party allegiance for the simple reason that they have a far, far higher allegiance which determines their action. But willingness to work [hard] will to a considerable extent compensate . . . in the eyes of most party leaders."[18] The same would apply to observant Jews or other people of conviction, whatever their background. Generally, leaders are both sensitive and understanding when such problems arise—though they continue to press for your vote. Party leaders are attempting to diminish chaos, and to enact programs while dealing with several hundred people, each of whom has strong views. Former Republican leader John Rhodes of Arizona said: "The average congressman of yesteryear was congenial, polite and willing to work with his colleagues whenever possible. . . . Today, a large number of congressmen are cynical, abrasive, frequently uncommunicative and ambitious to an inordinate degree. In their eagerness to draw attention to themselves—and advance politically—they frustrate the legislative process."[19] Leaders have a problem and so do members. Every legislator occasionally struggles to determine at what point you are disloyal to yourself when you are loyal to the party.

Complicating life for a legislator are those few members who are constantly devising schemes to exploit every situation for their party. Some simply have a hard time going directly from one point to another, and they see devilment behind every proposal made by a member of the opposition party. They are people who, if someone says "two and two equal four," will immediately ask themselves, "I wonder what he meant by that." They see schemes behind everything and they plan counterschemes constantly. My impression is that such efforts generally fail. Of course a political party must be wary of the opposition and not be played for fools. But if you deal openly, frankly, and with a minimum of partisan rhetoric, much can be accomplished and neither party loses. The Postsecondary Education Subcommittee, which I chair, has been able to handle a great deal of legislation, almost all of it with bipartisan support from subcommittee members. In part that is because of the caliber of such people as Representatives Tom Coleman of Missouri and James Jeffords of Vermont, both ranking Republicans. There are some in both parties in Congress who enjoy fighting more than getting a job done, and they contribute little; fortunately they are few in number.

There are many other party-related problems.

Because of the power of the presidency, no decision made by a political party is more important than whom it nominates every four years. Members of the House and Senate ordinarily know all the possible candidates reasonably well; they are in an excellent position to make a judgment, and in the parliamentary system they would make the judgment. In the United States it is politically safer not to take a stand, to avoid offending people in your state or district who are supporters of candidates other than the person you believe to be the best potential president. Do you owe the people the public expression of your judgment? Is it possible to quietly affect the result without taking a public stand?

Representative Berkley Bedell of Iowa, a widely respected Democratic member, faced a tough race for reelection in 1980. Three Republican members of the House from other states did television commercials for him. Then in 1982 he did a television commercial for a Republican member from Delaware and found himself the target of criticism from Democratic leaders. Should the Republican members have done the commercial for him? Should he have done the commercial for a Republican member? These are issues on which there are sharp divisions of opinion.

In one district a grand jury indicted a county official on charges of exposing himself to teenage girls who walked past his home. Facing reelection, party leaders tried to get him to withdraw; he refused, declaring his innocence. He had not been found guilty, but the evidence against him appeared to be strong. A candidate for Congress has an obligation to support the party so far as he or she can in good conscience, but how do you handle such a situation?

Being part of a ticket is somewhat akin to being an attorney for one side in a court battle. You have an obligation to present your side, honestly and truthfully, and then the jury (the voting public) makes the decision. In the middle of a trial, for an attorney suddenly to support the opposition would violate our system of jurisprudence. In a somewhat similar way, a candidate on one ticket should not under ordinary circumstances publicly support someone on another ticket. For the well-intentioned support of someone in another party easily leads to the "trading of candidates" by political leaders whose motives are not good, or simply buying support with cold, hard cash. The tradition of Democratic candidates avoiding public support of Republicans in an election, and Republicans avoiding public support of Democrats, is a fundamentally healthy restraint on the abuse of the political system. That does not mean a personal vote will be cast that way on a secret ballot. What if your party nominates someone for public office you believe to be incompetent or worse? If you simply pick and choose whom you publicly support, what does that do to the two-party political system?

Belonging to a political party cannot be all take and no give, any more than it can be with a church or a civic club. The problem in an election is more clear-cut than during a legislative session, where there is a tradition of relative independence. A member of Congress is not expected to vote with party leaders all the time; no one does. But where you draw the line, where you should resolve doubts in favor of your party, and where you should resolve them in favor of your instincts and your convictions is one of the ongoing dilemmas that members of Congress confront. Ultimately, the advice of Rutherford B. Hayes in his 1877 inaugural address is sound: "He serves the party best who serves the country best."[20] But the road that leads to that conclusion is not always smooth.

☆ **10** ☆

Balancing Self-restraint and Leadership

Everybody who has ever stood for anything that was any good has been accused of being a fanatic.

—Studs Terkel[1]

Our culture is in crisis today precisely because no creed, no symbol, no militant truth, is installed deeply enough now to help men constrain their capacity for expressing everything.

—Phillip Rieff[2]

Master Cromwell, you are now entered into the service of a most noble, wise and liberal prince; if you will follow my poor advice you shall, in your counsel-giving unto his Grace, ever tell him what he ought to do but never tell him what he is able to do. . . . For if the lion knew his own strength, hard were it for any man to rule him.

—Sir Thomas More, advice to his
successor as chancellor of England[3]

A retiring Republican from Ohio, Representative Charles Whalen, told me during his last months in the House: "I have voted for every reform that has come along. Individually I can defend each vote and tell you why it was both right and logical. But somehow cumulatively all of these reforms have resulted in a poorer legislative body."

He is right.

Drawing the line between what is needed for leadership and what is an expression of democracy is not easy. Nor is it always clear when taking a position is needed and desirable, and when self-restraint is more in order. Some of us in Congress take stands too frequently, some not often enough. Leaders can only be a reasonable distance ahead of their people, or they are no longer leaders; but leaders who only follow their people are leaders in name only. Those who wish to maintain leadership cannot lead on all issues. Real leadership includes "stepping on toes," and you can step on only so many toes before those who follow decide to change leaders. So choices must be made, both for reasons of political survival and for reasons of time. A legislator does not have the time to get involved in all prominent issues. Self-restraint is essential for effective leadership.

What is true for members of Congress also has validity for the public. Laws are designed to assist cooperative living, but society's conduct has a base in public sentiment that is more restricted than the extremity of the law; there is a general "this is the right thing to do" attitude that controls conduct. If every citizen attempted to come as close to violating the law as possible, freedom and our present system of self-governance would collapse. This morning I saw a woman walk in front of a car she did not see. Had the driver not tried hard to miss her he would have seriously injured her. Her responsibility for the accident would have been clear. But we function at a somewhat higher level of morality in society, not asking what the law demands, but what compassion, good sense, courtesy, and neighborliness demand. Most of us do not try to determine how much noise we can make in a theater or at a concert before we will be arrested; we do not stay seated when the "Star Spangled Banner" is played, though it would be legal to do so. If we did everything the law permitted, stretched our conduct as close to lawlessness as possible, the result would be chaos. Thucydides, explaining to ancient Athenians how their system worked, noted: "We obey those unwritten laws which it is an acknowledged shame to break."[4] That remains true today. We are circumscribed by traditions and attitudes that often have stronger impact than the law. Historians Will and Ariel Durant have observed: "The Englishman does not so much make English civilization as it makes him; if he carries it wherever he goes, and dresses for dinner in Timbuktu, it is not that he is creating his civilization there anew, but that he acknowledges even there its mastery over his soul."[5] We are all restrained to some degree by a heritage and custom that makes freedom possible.

Let me give you an illustration of where the American public's conduct and the U.S. official's conduct intersect. After a presidential election the defeated candidate congratulates the winner, although his sentiments may be considerably different than those expressed publicly. When Richard Nixon narrowly lost to John Kennedy and Hubert Humphrey narrowly lost to Richard Nixon, the losers congratulated the winners as soon as the outcome became clear. It would have been legal for each of the losers to refrain from doing so; it would have been legal for each to point to deficiencies in the election process and ask his supporters to march in a public demonstration in every community in the nation; and it would have been legal for such demonstrations to take place. The result, however, would be a significantly weakened democracy. Instead, losers who have any sense at all of how our system works, congratulate winners, whether it is for a city council seat or for the presidency. The public does not take to the streets. Many do not like the election results, but there is a remarkably smooth transition of power at all levels of government.

Even the restraints members place upon themselves in debate help to keep the system running smoothly. "My distinguished colleague, who has provided important leadership in so many areas, is completely wrong on this one" is the type of oft-repeated oratorical flourish that may sound unctuous or strange to someone sitting in the gallery or watching on television, but it softens the disagreement, modifies the tone, and serves all of us well. The ceremonies at an inauguration or a State of the Union address are an important part of that exercise of self-restraint. Both parties are present, and all of us stand and applaud the president. "He is our leader," we say, even though we may strongly disagree with what he says. These "small things" are imporant in permitting the system to function. There is a general, unexpressed recognition that self-restraint is essential if society is to serve all of us well. This need is greater in the United States than in some countries, for we are a nation whose diversity in racial, ethnic, and religious groups can be either a cause of enrichment or the source of division, misunderstanding, and violence. In many nations—Japan, for example—a dispute between two individuals almost always remains that; in the United States it can, in the wrong setting, cause racial, ethnic, or religious violence.

Leadership and an inflated sense of self-importance sometimes get confused, a temptation to which those of us who receive attention from the public and the press can easily succumb. Theologian Jerald C. Brauer wrote: "Americans are convinced they are a chosen people. Providence has selected them for a special task."[6] If that is accepted, and if you are one of the leaders of that nation, an inflated posture easily results. President U. S. Grant said of a Massachusetts senator: "The reason Sumner doesn't believe in the Bible is because he didn't write it himself."[7] Humility and greatness generally go hand in hand. I find a swollen sense of self-importance uncommon in the House and Senate, but it does on occasion assert itself, to no one's credit.

Sometimes self-restraint is camouflage for indifference or laziness. "Playing it safe" is not a description those of us in Congress would like applied to our activities; self-restraint sounds much better. Distinguishing within yourself what is self-restraint and what is political cowardice is not easy; we usually manage to assign the better motivations to ourselves. I. F. Stone told a small group of House members: "The most powerful force in this town [Washington, D.C.] is inertia."[8] We are so "politically prudent" or "gutless" or "restrained"—you choose the word—that far too often real needs in this nation are ignored. Strictly from the viewpoint of winning elections, ignoring needs is generally safer than facing them, avoiding new ideas safer than probing them. On October 7, 1930, the *New York World* gave this advice to politicians:

> New thoughts excite
> The voters' dread.
> Be sure you're trite,
> And go ahead.

There is another dimension to the problem, however. Representative Les AuCoin, a Democrat from Oregon, told the *New York Times* during Gerald Ford's presidency:

A committee of 435 cannot run the country—and an intensely political committee of 435 egos surely cannot. No one dislikes the policies of the last seven years of GOP Administrations more than I do. But the way to change that is to recapture the White House rather than attempt to make Congress something which, inherently, it cannot be. Sooner or later the Democrats will again control the White House. We will have won a hollow victory if we have structurally weakened what still is the best instrument for leadership in this country.[9]

It is politically easy for Democrats in Congress to restrict a Republican president; it is easy for Republicans to do the same to a Democratic president. Sometimes those restrictions are not a healthy exercise of the balance of powers, but unnecessary impositions that reduce the effectiveness of the presidency. That applies not only to the presidential-congressional relationship, but to the relationship between leaders and members in the House and Senate. A blissful assumption that the democratic processes will automatically correct flaws in our society, that effective leadership is not needed, is a misreading of both the past and the present. The saying "The Lord protects Americans and drunks" may have an appealing ring, but it is not a defense of misusing either alcohol or democracy.[10] For the U.S. system of government to work, elected leaders in both the administrative and legislative branches must have the effective tools, must have some muscle. The nation needs leaders, but it also needs those in Congress who are willing to follow, who will not desert a cause if three letters arrive from the district showing disagreement, or if the chance to stray from leadership presents an opportunity for a television appearance.

On the other hand, there must be people willing to stand up when things go wrong, who are willing to say unpopular things, who are willing to risk disapproval. Early in this century one of the most colorful labor leaders, Mary Jones, better known as Mother Jones, talked tough: "I am not afraid of the press or the militia. I would fight God Almighty himself if he didn't play square with me."[11] A West Virginia prosecutor said of her: "There sits the most dangerous woman in America. She comes into a

state where peace and prosperity reign. She crooks her finger—
20,000 contented men lay down their tools and walk out."[12] The
nation could not absorb too many like Mother Jones, but she
provided courage and bold leadership in a nation that needed
it; and someone had to stand up to the massive abuses against
the miners during that period. Senator Joseph McCarthy fright-
ened a nation, as well as those who should have defended
the rights of their fellow citizens. The United States needed the
courageous Senator William Benton of Connecticut to lead the
way by introducing a resolution of censure to stop McCarthy.
When Franklin D. Roosevelt misused his authority to herd Jap-
anese-Americans into internment camps during World War II—
to the nation's shame—there were unfortunately only a few scattered voices of opposition. Ambassador George F. Kennan received sharp criticism when he became the first major U.S. voice
at the end of World War II to warn against identifying too closely
with the Soviets, to be wary of their government. Years later,
after many changes in top Soviet leadership, he warned against
drifting too far from the Soviets, into a position of excessively
negative reaction to their every move. Again, his statement evoked
criticism. My guess is that history will judge him correct in both
instances. A man of much greater knowledge and insight than
most, he had—and has—an obligation to speak out, to lead. More
lives would have been lost in Vietnam had not a few members
of the House and Senate been willing to speak out, to risk censure
by the public, their colleagues, and the president.

Often there is also the opportunity to mesh leadership and
followership quietly in ways that will produce not publicity but
results. This gets action without reinforcing a public image of
constant conflict. As Will Durant noted: "Order is the mother of
civilization and liberty; chaos is the midwife of dictatorship."[13]
Our nation is neither threatened by dictatorship nor in the throes
of chaos, but when people can effectively and quietly work together to achieve laudable ends, democracy is strengthened and
the dangers that can threaten any system are diminished. Chinese
philosopher and poet Lao-tse observed: "Of the best rulers, the
people [only] know that they exist . . . [and] when their task is
accomplished . . . the people all remark, 'We have done it ourselves.' "[14] That is often not possible; it takes good leaders and

good followers. Leaders sometimes have to choose between getting a job done and getting credit.

A House member came to me recently to discuss a measure to be voted on: "I am in a real bind. During the campaign I pledged to vote against this, but now that I see all sides of the issue I'm convinced I was wrong. If I vote for it editorials will attack me for lying during the campaign, and people will lose confidence in me and in the system. But I will hate myself if I vote against it." Most members have found themselves in that dilemma at one time or another.

As I write this, I have introduced a bill that would be of substantial assistance to the poor of the nation; but one of the AFL-CIO leaders indicated to me that they would oppose it. My immediate reaction was incredulity, then fury, that people who represent themselves as protectors of the underdogs in our society should take such a stand. At first I thought about issuing a statement blasting them. On second thought, I decided I should talk to more leaders, to see if I could get them to turn around, remembering that on more than one occasion I also have been wrong in my initial reaction to legislation. Whether or not this will work I do not know. A second meeting with two AFL-CIO leaders now makes prospects look more promising. If I had criticized the AFL-CIO I could have made national news and appeared on network television (modesty is not one of the virtues of politicians), and I could have pleased some of my constituents who think I'm too closely aligned with labor. But I probably would have doomed my bill's chances. Sometimes what I do upon reflection is not as good as what I do upon impulse, but usually it is better. This is the type of personal struggle that my colleagues and I go through daily. It may be described in a variety of ways, but it ultimately comes down to the choice of how much visible leadership a member should provide and how much self-restraint. The public is entitled to know what is going on and how laws are made, and to win elections members also have to be visible. But to get a bill passed, quiet conversation with a few people on a committee, or with a few lobbyists, usually does more good than an appearance on national television. Where you draw the line differs from day to day, from decision to decision.

In a variety of personal ways the choice is made between leadership and self-restraint: in campaign style, in how often you speak on the floor, in how letters are answered. I tell those few candidates or newcomers to Congress who come to me for advice to be true to themselves; do what you feel comfortable doing; don't let the public relations people manipulate you. During the Republican convention of 1960, John F. Kennedy watched while Nixon accepted the cheers of the delegates. Kennedy turned to those watching with him and said: "If I have to stand up before a crowd and wave both of my arms above my head like that in order to become President of the United States, I'll never make it."[15] Obviously, there is nothing immoral about throwing your hands in the air, but candidates and office holders are wise to follow their instincts, not the opinion molders. If someone suggests that you lead a five-mile hike, and you detest hiking, don't do it. If the public relations people want you to wrap the American flag around your personal political views, be careful. Remember the words of French observer Alexis de Tocqueville in speaking of the U.S. scene: "It is impossible to conceive a more . . . garrulous patriotism; it wearies even those who are disposed to respect it."[16] People sense misuse. For all of its imperfections, one of the good things that generally occurs in our democracy is that people sooner or later understand whether a politician is genuine. It is communicated in a variety of small ways. Office holders must not only restrain themselves, but those around them, so that the public sees the real thing, not some immediately appealing but artificially created product. A counterfeit bill may be accepted once or twice, but not often.

There are no rigid rules to follow in determining what to do and what not to do, when to practice self-restraint and when to provide visible leadership. But it is important that those in Congress—and the public—have some sense of the dimensions of the problem, have some understanding that a strong dose of common sense is needed for a democracy to function.

☆ **11** ☆

The God of Public Opinion

In the new politics . . . the people or region are carefully surveyed not to determine their needs or aspirations, but to assess their fears, hates and prejudices and then an expensive propaganda campaign is tailor-made to exploit the worst in them.

—Senator Albert Gore, Sr.[1]

Our elected representatives, and the "communications" experts they employ, study and analyze public attitudes by sophisticated new techniques, but their purpose has little to do with leadership, still less with education. Their purpose, it seems, is to discover what people want and fear and dislike, and to identify themselves with those sentiments. They seek to discover which issues can be safely emphasized and which are more prudently avoided. This approach to politics is the opposite of leadership; it is followership, for purposes of self-advancement.

—Senator J. William Fulbright[2]

It is hard to look up to a leader who keeps his ear to the ground.

—James H. Boren[3]

The worship of false gods has been a problem for humanity from its earliest days, but for the lawmaker there is no idol at whose shrine there is more temptation to kneel than the god of public opinion. Those who worship at this shrine receive tangible results: they are elected and reelected. Total obeisance to this god will do great harm to the nation in the long run, but most of us who hold public office have a tendency to deceive ourselves into believing that whatever gets us elected is in the best interest of the country, even if it requires stifling conscience.

Although the strength of public opinion has been magnified and refined in recent years, it is not a new phenomenon. More than a century before the American Revolution, the French philosopher and mathematician Pascal wrote: "It would be a strange miracle if infallibility existed in one man. But it appears so natural for it to reside in a multitude, since the conduct of God is hidden under nature. . . ."[4] Many centuries earlier Plato criticized those who "teach nothing but the opinion of the many" and added:

> I might compare them to a man who should study the tempers and desires of a mighty strong beast who is fed by him—he would learn how to approach and handle him, also at what times and from what causes he is dangerous or . . . is soothed or infuriated; and you may suppose further, that when, by continually attending upon him, he has become perfect in all this, he calls knowledge wisdom . . . although he has no real notion of what he means by the principles or passions of which he is speaking, but calls this honourable and that dishonourable, or good or evil, or just or unjust, all in accordance with the tastes and tempers of the great brute. Good he pronounces to be that in which the beast delights and evil to be that which he dislikes.[5]

That is uncomfortably close to where we are today. More and more members of the House and Senate are elected after they have taken polls and then followed the dictates of the results rather than their own inclinations and convictions, if they have any. Polling replaces investigating what the national needs are and trying to meet those needs. Regrettably, in recent years the White House, under both political parties, has suffered from the same hypnotic spell.

"I'll do what you want me to do" sounds great in a speech in the home district. People like to hear it. No politician is going to ignore public opinion. We are always aware of it. But that may not be what the nation needs. For example, a substantial portion of the medicine this economy should have is not popular. Do we prescribe what is best for the economy or best for our political hides? The easy answer is the latter. Even the defenders of adherence to public opinion acknowledge that it should be "*genuine* public opinion," meaning that it is the "lasting, considered, mature judgment of the people," not an easy thing to discover in the hectic pace of a lawmaker.[6]

More than a century ago John Stuart Mill wrote: "When the opinion of masses of merely average men are everywhere become or becoming the dominant power . . . it is in these circumstances most especially, that exceptional individuals . . . should be encouraged in acting differently from the mass."[7] Almost two thousand years earlier the biographer Plutarch observed:

> For this is indeed the true condition of men in public life, who, to gain the vain title of being the people's leaders and governors, are content to make themselves the slaves and followers of all the people's humours and caprices. . . . These men, steered . . . by popular applause, though they bear the name of governors, are in reality the mere underlings of the multitude. . . . As Phocion answered King Antipater, who sought his approbation of some unworthy action, "I cannot be your flatterer and your friend," so these men should answer the people, "I cannot govern and obey you."[8]

The two worst influences on law making today are the way in which we finance campaigns and the polling that results in a legislative body tossed about by the whims of public opinion. There is nothing wrong with a candidate for public office taking polls. Any sensible candidate for a major office will do so. But to use polls to determine what stand to take on issues is an abuse that has become all too common.

I do not agree with Cicero's statement: "In the common people there is no wisdom, no penetration, no power of judgment."[9] For with the common people there is often wisdom, a sense of justice, and a keener awareness of the problems of society than exists in the seat of government. To recognize the problems that these people sense is one thing; to assume there is some way to listen to them in order to find the answers to complex problems is quite another.

How could the nation find itself today with deficits over $200 billion for one fiscal year when we elected a president who said he would be balancing the budget this same fiscal year? Part of it can be attributed to economic theories drawn on a restaurant napkin. But a good portion of it is because Congress and the administration did exactly what the public wanted: we reduced taxes significantly (supported by the polls); we markedly increased defense spending (supported by the polls); and we cut back on programs for the poor (supported by the polls). That someone's economic theories appeared to justify popular opinion made it even nicer. We could give the people everything they want and at the same time reduce deficits (supported by the polls). But public opinion did not equate with sound economics. Now we are in an economic mess; we have taken some tentative steps to extricate ourselves, but it is politically awkward for all concerned.

The Panama Canal Treaty came dangerously close to not being approved by the Senate. The issue was never the merits of the case. Yes, a few senators genuinely objected to it, but a secret vote would have resulted in perhaps a 90–10 vote of approval. Were it not for the courage of someone like Republican Senator Henry Bellmon of Oklahoma who supported the treaty—and later announced he would not seek reelection—we would have had serious troubles on our hands in Central America, far worse than our present problems. Former Senator Joseph H. Ball has written: "Few successful politicians are crusaders by nature. Very often they march in parades, particularly the popular ones, but rarely do they lead them."[10] The nation needs people willing to lead.

Where are the men and women of courage and conviction, the "profiles in courage" to which we like to point in history? Many of them are "back home." They appeared on the scene, but we found them too controversial, and so anemic, inoffensive substitutes were found. Their substitutes took polls regularly and followed them faithfully; what the polls said to do on abortion and disarmament they did, fudging a little on the latter to get some campaign contributions; when the polls said, "praise the president," they did; when the polls said sneeze, they sneezed. They had slick television commercials that showed their thinking to be totally in line with the people whose votes they needed.

They got elected. They are in office today, taking polls to determine how they should vote. When they have to vote on a major issue on which their staffs have not had a chance to survey, they get fidgety, break into a cold sweat before and after they vote. Their families take great pride in the fact that they are national leaders. Their influence, outside of their votes, is about as great as that of a page, who runs errands.

This may be an exaggeration, but it comes far too close to describing too many legislators. I do not suggest that all members of the House and Senate blindly follow public opinion, but more do than should, and the nation is generally ill served in the process. Polls do, however, provide citizens a chance to balance slightly the serious flaws in our system of deciding issues through campaign financing. But sometimes public opinion compounds the problem, for the same groups that have the money to finance campaigns often have the money to simulate grass-roots support on an issue. I do not suggest that public opinion should be ignored; it will not, it cannot be. The public wants justice; the public wants to see hungry people fed and the poor given greater opportunities; the public wants peace. But sometimes these basic desires are in conflict with other thrusts of public opinion. The public cannot study a tax bill or a federal budget in detail; the citizenry cannot measure the help or devastation a measure may have on the lives of a host of people, and they may be deceived as to the impact and intent of measures. It is at this point that courage is needed, and too often is lacking.

☆ 12 ☆

The Media

The press never quotes me correctly unless I say something
stupid.
—a Missouri official[1]

The American newspaper today is one of the chief enemies
of the Kingdom of God.
—Resolution of the Northwest Conference
of the Methodist Episcopal Church, 1933[2]

Because television is the arbiter of the significant, little can
succeed without its blessing.
—Daniel Schorr[3]

My office has standing instructions: reporters get priority.
That is true of virtually all House and Senate offices. It
is but one small indication of the importance members place on
the media. Reporters help to shape our image to our constituents;
they determine for the nation what portion of our debates are
worth noting, what arguments have merit. If the newspapers,
radio, and television play up an issue, it becomes important simply for the time that issue will take in our office, whether it is
intrinsically important or not. "The media runs Congress like
the railroads used to run state legislative bodies," one of my
colleagues claims. That is an exaggeration containing a kernel
of truth. Representative David Obey of Wisconsin has written:
"Both the political profession and the news profession have the
same potential weakness. We both need public approval to survive."[4] A reporter yearns to see that byline, the public official the

story about himself or herself. Representative Jim Wright said: "Public office is awfully hard on humility."[5] People in the public eye easily get an exaggerated view of their own importance and of the virtue of their actions. Even the prophet Isaiah said: "My bowels shall sound like an harp," a slight exaggeration.[6] The media are the reassurance of our importance, and the key to our importance, both at the same time. What are the strengths and weaknesses of the media on the Washington scene? To what extent should a legislator play up to the media? Are there long-range threats to freedom of the press that should concern us?

Washington, D.C., has more quality reporters per capita than any city in the world. The nature of the decision-making process in Washington attracts them. Just as Washington is the mecca for most politicians, so it is for most journalists. The same process that moves politicians from the city council to the state legislature to Washington moves reporters from the police beat to covering state government to covering the nation's capital. Some politicians avoid the process just as some reporters do; but most would like to follow it.

Reporters look to Congress and see our faults, usually with a fair amount of accuracy and discernment. As a former newsman now serving in Congress, let me suggest what I sense are the five basic weaknesses of congressional coverage.

1. *Trivial items often get more attention than matters of substance.*

A few days ago I walked from my office to the Capitol and saw a large gathering of television cameras and reporters. I assumed it was a major head of state and the visit somehow hadn't been brought to my attention. I asked one of the reporters who it was. He responded: "[Representative] Jim Wright lost a bet to [Representative] Walter Fauntroy on the Dallas-Washington game, and Wright will be pushing Fauntroy in a wheelbarrow and then have a brief press conference about it." I watched it on network television that night.

During my service in the state legislature Senator Paul Douglas called one day and asked me to introduce a resolution in the Illinois General Assembly urging the U.S. Congress to make the corn tassel the national flower. He would then introduce the measure in the Senate. Because of my great admiration for him

I immediately said yes. But as I reflected on it I thought more and more that I really did not want to do that, a non-substantial type of thing with which I felt uncomfortable. That night I called the senator and asked, "Are you sure you want me to introduce a resolution on the corn tassel? Are you sure you want to introduce a resolution in the Senate?" The professor-turned-senator laughed and responded with a lecture that taught me something about politics and journalism.

"Paul," he said, "if you want to stay in public office you have to get media attention. The substantial things you do generally will not get attention unless they are involved in a major controversy. But the media loves trivia. You have to do a certain amount of that to stay alive politically. No one will get angry with you because you want to make the corn tassel the national flower. And don't worry; it will never pass."

There is nothing intrinsically wrong with a bet on a football game, or introducing a resolution on the corn tassel. But the knowledge by policy makers that more attention to silliness and less to substance pays off politically does not help the political process and does not elevate the American public.

A part of the same problem is personality-oriented reporting. Dennis Farney of the *Wall Street Journal* comments: "Press coverage of ideas is bad. It takes much more work to dig into a story on ideas and so we tend to deal in personalities."[7] More Americans can tell you that President Gerald Ford occasionally stumbled physically than have any idea about Gerald Ford's role in the Salt I agreement with the Soviets. Reporters, pressed for time, are attracted to the obvious, to the easy story, to the story that is more likely to be read than to the story that will inform.

Cable television coverage of House proceedings has helped somewhat to place more focus on the issues. The audience is small, but I am always pleased—and a little surprised—to meet people who have tuned in. They emerge with greater understanding of both the process and the issues.

2. *There is an appalling insensitivity to the international dimension in both stories and editorials.*

One of the nation's major foundations recently held a "think tank" session on what it should do in the future to help the nation. One of my suggestions: arrange for reporters, editorial writers, publishers, and media executives to travel and learn more about the world. In his book *Megatrends,* John Naisbitt notes that the London *Economist* has "a global view almost always more balanced than that of the American media."[8] That comment says more about U.S. media than it does about the *Economist.*

In front of me is a picture from a major U.S. newspaper with an Associated Press wirephoto credit. The picture shows Chinese citizens paying tribute to a government leader who has died. The caption reads: "Peking peasants pay last respects to . . ."[9] Can you imagine any U.S. newspaper showing a group of our citizens paying homage to a dead official commencing with these words: "U.S. peasants pay last respects . . ."? The caption was not meant to be malicious; a small putdown, it is one of many we inflict on people from other countries.

After the seizure of American hostages in Iran, there were few stories that showed any comprehension whatsoever of the religious dimensions of the problem in that country, for reporters and editors—like those of us in public office and virtually all U.S. citizens—had little understanding of the Moslem world.

In a series of public television shows on the media, former newspaper publisher Hodding Carter made this observation about Soviet coverage: "The three networks, CBS, NBC, and ABC, averaged only an hour apiece in their evening news coverage from Moscow in all of 1982. By contrast, one West German television network carried as much coverage from Russia as all three American networks combined. As a result, American prime time TV news offered few stories about such essential topics as the Soviet economy. Taken together, NBC, ABC, and CBS devoted less than half an hour to the subject in 1982."[10]

After serving in the U.S. Senate and losing a tight race for governor of Illinois, Adlai E. Stevenson III responded to a question about the media in Washington: "I see a young generation [of reporters] that . . . too often sees successful journalism as requiring sensationalism and superficiality. I just don't see the serious reporting of events in the world that I was familiar with in the 1950s and 1960s."[11]

Walter Laquer wrote in the June 1983 *Washington Journalism Review* that foreign news coverage is definitely not as good as in most other countries that have a free press. . . . The number of foreign correspondents abroad has fallen from 515 in 1963 to 429 in 1975 and is now probably not larger than 350. . . . The neglect of foreign news and the low quality of comment has political consequences: American public opinion is by and large less well informed about world affairs than public opinion elsewhere and this is also true for elite opinion.

One of the subjects most poorly covered is congressional foreign travel. The assumption that foreign travel is an abuse of public privilege is near the surface of most stories. Where there is abuse of public travel it should be covered and denounced, but most congressional foreign travel is not abused.

The great public disservice by members of Congress is not traveling enough, with members voting on issues important to the future of this nation and other nations when they have little background for those decisions. *I have yet to see a news article or editorial criticizing any member of Congress for not traveling, yet that is by far the greater abuse.* I have had dozens of colleagues tell me they would like to travel in order to understand some area of the world better, but they fear the kind of news coverage and editorial criticism they will receive. There is absolutely no fear of criticism for not traveling, for as far as I know that criticism has never occurred. I have seen campaign literature pointing out that in twelve years in Congress a member has never been outside the United States. Are there no editorial writers anywhere who fear a Congress made up of people with such limited experience of the world?

What if before our involvement in Vietnam there had been ten members of the House and Senate who had had the courage to visit there despite the editorial and reportorial barbs they would have received? There is at least the slim possibility that war would have been prevented and fifty-seven thousand American lives and three million Asian lives could have been saved. If editorials had been urging travel rather than discouraging it, some members might have gone there.

No member of the House or Senate should fail to visit the

Soviet Union at least once every five years, to have some minimal understanding of the strengths and defects of their system and to establish some personal contacts with leaders there. But where are the editorial voices suggesting that? I hear or read none.

A member of Congress who makes decisions that affect his or her district without visiting that district is irresponsible; but the irresponsibility of making decisions that have an impact on the survival of the human race without attempting to understand other nations and other people has not penetrated the editorial and reportorial sector adequately, if at all. When it does, there can also be reporting on the imbalance in foreign congressional travel. For the last two years for which complete information is available (1979–80) members of the House and Senate made 136 trips to Great Britain, 99 to France, 105 to West Germany, 43 to the Soviet Union, but none at all to Bangladesh, Bolivia, Chile, Ghana, Libya, Uruguay, or 55 other nations. There is no country that is so unimportant that it should be ignored by members of the House and Senate. I do not suggest that the major European nations should not be visited more frequently than others, but our inattention to many of the developing nations is shortsighted. El Salvador, for the years 1979 and 1980, had a grand total of one visitor. The imbalance of congressional travel is something those of us in Congress, and those who cover Congress, should rectify.

The lack of congressional travel is something that the news media throughout the nation must help rectify. Unlike the newspaper and media situation in Britain and France, where a few publications and stations reach the bulk of the population, we are a nation with scattered news sources. Yes, the networks and the wire services do penetrate nationally, but editorially there is no such concentrated voice. On balance, that is a good thing, but it does mean that those who write editorials in remote corners of the nation have a greater responsibility in the United States.

One of the finest editors this nation has produced, Irving Dilliard of the *St. Louis Post-Dispatch,* gave a lecture in honor of the memory of another great editor, William Allan White, on the topic "The Editor I Wish I Were." It included these words: "He travels in distant as well as neighboring countries. He knows that he must write about far away places and he must print news concerning them. And he knows that peoples overseas will seem less strange and their decisions and reactions to us less peculiar if he has met them in their home lands. He knows that travel helps him to understand and that understanding is fundamental to his work as an editor."[12] Fred Starr, president of Oberlin College, has written: "Few American newspapers print more than three columns of foreign news during an entire week. . . . The cultural isolationism that our physical separation from other nations once fostered has been perpetuated in a world of instant communication and interdependence."[13]

3. *Political commentators lack a sense of perspective.*

Richard Strout, now eighty-five years old and recently retired, had perspective in his TRB column in the *New Republic*. Time and an acute sense of observation combined to give him that gift. Among the major columnists, George Will provides perspective frequently. So does David Broder. Joseph Kraft, Tom Wicker, Colman McCarthy, Anthony Lewis, and James Reston occasionally sit back and look at the large scene and write more reflectively. Others could be cited as well. Perhaps it is simply that the years have gilded my memory of Walter Lippmann's work, but I want to read the thoughts of those who have some sense of history and what life is all about, who have not simply raced from a press conference and, still panting, deliver more details than I received from the wire service story on the same event. In an age of television, with the sense of immediacy it provides, perspective is needed even more than at the height of Lippmann's influence. I yearn for the column that seems to come from someone with a cabin in the woods, who read Plato this morning as well as the morning newspapers, who stands in awe both of humanity's ability to destroy itself and of the trees that surround him or her, whose vision and understanding go beyond the nearest traffic light. I cannot define exactly what I seek because I do not know exactly what it is; I only know that I miss it.

4. *Editorials are too flabby.*

There are few, if any, newspaper editorials I disagree with more regularly than those of the *St. Louis Globe-Democrat*. They automatically attack almost any proposal that will help poor people, and automatically praise almost anything carrying the label defense, no matter how wasteful. But these editorials have punch. There is no question where the editors stand. When I vote against an MX missile I know that their newspaper will attack me by name. Its vigorous positions, whether you agree or not, should be applauded.

Television and radio offer the worst examples of weak editorials. I heard one the other day urging citizens to keep the streets clean, followed by the announcement: "Anyone with an opposing viewpoint may contact . . ." Television editorials too often fit Frank Lloyd Wright's description of television: "chewing gum for the eyes."[14]

Editorials should make clear where the journal or station stands, but if there is an unwillingness to tackle the tough issues, forget the editorials. Newspaper editorials that call for a specific committee to do something ought to list the committee members in the editorial. Then there should be a follow-up editorial listing how the members voted, commending those who voted "correctly" and criticizing those who voted incorrectly. Yet that seldom happens. There rarely is editorial "follow-through."

Editorials also suffer from being too depersonalized. Surveys show that columnists are read more than editorials, that letters to the editor are read more than editorials. I read Stephen Rosenfeld's weekly column in the *Washington Post* more carefully than the editorials in the same newspaper, even though I know he is also one of the editorial writers, because I have some sense of who is writing his column, what he believes. I cannot identify with an amorphous blob called "we" in an editorial. In the days of Horace Greeley, Charles Dana, James Gordon Bennett, and Joseph Pulitzer, editorial pages flamed with indignation or praise. Sometimes they lacked balance. But readers knew who was speaking. I want balance, but I also want to know who is writing. I want some righteous indignation and writing that is so clear a fifth-grader can understand the point—or even a member of Congress.

H. L. Mencken, when asked for his suggestions for the editorial page of the *Baltimore Sun*, responded: "In journalism, it seems to me, it is far better to be wrong than to be timorous. The papers that get attention are those that take a positive line, and stick to it with tenacity. . . . I recommend that a steady increase in editorial vigor be made a matter of fixed policy."[15]

5. *Journalists need to keep alive at least a small flame of optimism.*
Whiskey is not the only downfall of many reporters; cynicism is another. A questioning attitude and a healthy skepticism are important tools of the trade for a reporter. But sometimes they spill over into a bitterness, a belief that humanity can produce nothing worthwhile, at least the humanity that holds public office. Just as reporters who drink too much ordinarily don't get ahead, it has been my observation that journalists who imbibe too much of cynicism have limited upward mobility. A good journalist ought to be able to become enthusiastic about some things. Journalists should be people in whom there is at least a flicker of hope.

Two other concerns about the media that do not involve reporters are (1) the increasing postage rates, which discourage the dissemination of ideas by print and encourage excessive reliance on radio and television as information sources; and (2) the increasing concentration of newspaper ownership in the hands of fewer and fewer people.

The first problem can be corrected whenever Congress has the will to do so; but unless lawmakers recognize high postage rates as a serious infringement of the free flow of ideas, this problem will get worse. The nation will be forced to depend on thirty-second television analyses of complex problems. In 1981 the postage bill for the *Christian Century* was $60,000; it was $120,000 one year later. The *United Methodist Reporter*'s bill jumped 154 percent; the *American Legion* magazine's went up 75 percent, up $1 million. Newspapers charged their mail subscribers more money to pay for the added postage, and circulation dropped. The net result: more and more citizens with less and less in-depth information and viewpoints.

The second problem is much more complicated and I see no easy solution. It is not likely to be seriously addressed until a tangible, comprehensible misuse of the concentration of media power takes place, perhaps within the next few years. The problem of failing newspapers is not a new one in our country. Of

the 2,120 newspapers established up to 1820, only thirty-four
lasted a generation. But the concentration of newspaper ownership is a new phenomenon. It is compounded by another reality: in 1910 60 percent of our nation's cities had competing
newspapers; now fewer than 3 percent do. Sweden, with a population roughly that of New York City, has four hundred daily
newspapers. In 1826 the United States had almost twice as many
newspaper readers for each thousand citizens as Great Britain;
now the opposite is true. Up to now the newspaper chains in the
United States have generally acted responsibly, often improving
the locally published product; but the aim too often is only profit.
I shudder when I read the following statement by an executive
of a newspaper chain: "Never get more than ten degrees ahead
of the public, and you can be assured of a steady ten percent
profit."[16] Change the word *profit* to the phrase *vote margin* and
many of my colleagues in Congress would say the same. The
head of one of the nation's largest newspaper chains advised
editors that a paper's "editorial policy should generally be kept
in tune with prevailing public opinion."[17] My impression is that
neither editors nor reporters need such admonitions. There is
already an ample supply of timidity among them. Too many
reporters who cover Washington look around to see what others
are writing and then say essentially the same thing. Newspapers—and legislators—ought to provide more courageous leadership, and I fear chain ownership diminishes that possibility.

But what happens when—not if—foreign corporations buy
some of the large chains? What happens when Mobil or General
Motors takes over a chain? In 1932 Germany published more
newspapers than any industrialized nation, but a study of journalism during Hitler's rise to power notes: "A distinctive weakness of the German press manifested itself . . . when banks,
industrial firms, and other economic interests began to participate in the ownership of the newspapers."[18]

A Democratic caucus has been held, and after we emerge the
phone rings. A reporter wants to know what went on. Having
been a reporter once, I scrupulously avoid being the source for
such stories; my journalistic background makes me suspect to

some of my colleagues. But I know that any enterprising reporter will get the story; generally, secret meetings remain about as secret as a presidential press conference. Members have a problem deciding what to reveal and what not to reveal; what would be disloyalty to a colleague and what would be denial to the media and the public of the knowledge of what and how government decisions are being made. For these questions there are no precise answers.

There are other dilemmas. A reporter calls from one of the "grocery store weeklies" that sensationalize with little regard for th truth. Should a member give an interview? Or another problem: sometimes it is difficult to get enough members to attend a committee meeting without the assurance of television coverage. Should you schedule a "star," who may have little to say of substance, in order to get members there—entice them through television coverage to hear the more substantial witnesses? Television reporter Daniel Schorr relates running into Senator Hubert Humphrey trying to get members for a Joint Congressional Economic Committee hearing: "Half-jokingly, half-despairingly, he asked if I could install dummy cameras and turn on some bright lights to attract truant members of his committee."[19]

One temptation the lawmaker should not succumb to is letting the media determine policy. Read the editorials and reflect on them; if they are right follow them. But the threat of bad publicity or the lure of good publicity should not cause a legislator to depart from sound policy. That is easy to say, but sometimes hard to do. The extreme example of this came in the last century when William Randolph Hearst sent artist Frederic Remington to Cuba to draw sketches of "the war." When Remington got there he found no fighting and cabled Hearst that there was no war and he planned to come home. Hearst cabled back: "Please remain. You furnish the pictures, and I'll furnish the war."[20] When a U.S. ship, the *Maine,* was sunk, Hearst's *New York Journal,* which had been advocating war with Spain, stirred passions with less than accurate reporting. Three days after the sinking, the *Journal's* headline read: "THE WHOLE Country THRILLS WITH WAR FEVER."[21] I am sure that standing up to William Randolph Hearst and the public opinion he had influenced was not easy, illustrated by the fact that few did it. But viewed from the comfortable distance of more than eight decades, the responsibility to do so was clear.

Almost a century and a half ago American author James Fenimore Cooper observed: "The press, like fire, is an excellent servant, but a terrible master."[22] That remains true, but where to draw the line, and how to draw the line, is a dilemma for the lawmaker.

☆ 13 ☆

Conclusion

People are always extolling the man of principles; but I think
the superior man is one who knows that he must find his way
in a maze of principles.
                                    —Justice Oliver Wendell Holmes[1]

The more that comes out the better. It's the only way to make
politicians real. . . . If we can't accept them as they are then
we really are going to [have to] take a hard look at ourselves.
                          —Self-proclaimed paramour of a president[2]

Fastidiousness is a virtue in literature and an impossibility in
politics.
                                                    —George Will[3]

"**G**et ready for the most important offer of all time," boomed
the announcer during a television commercial one January morning. I soon learned that "the most important offer of
all time" would provide me with a "gold necklace" for $19.95.[4]
The promise to produce more than is delivered is a weakness
not only of television, but of politics in any free system. Those
interested in the moral dimensions of politics should be particularly careful not to exaggerate the impact of the attempts to
apply moral absolutes to policy decision making. Woodrow Wilson could advise us on that.

The practical dilemmas that real-life politicians face do not fit
into easily wrapped packages to which moral labels can be at-
tached. This has led some to suggest that ethics and politics must
be divorced completely, a notion I hear espoused occasionally
by theoreticians on college campuses but not by practical poli-

ticians who know better. Churchill worte: "A nation without conscience is a nation without a soul. A nation without a soul is a
nation that cannot live."[5] Morality helps shape the goals toward
which we must strive and limits the means that can be used in
reaching those goals. The goals generally must be loftier than
the means. War is not an acceptable moral goal, but war as a
means to achieve a goal (for example, the Afghan resistance to
the Soviet presence in their country) is often recognized as morally acceptable, though sentiment on that is changing. Putting
people in prison is not an acceptable goal, but putting people in
prison as a means of achieving a stable society somewhat more
free of crime is considered acceptable. Unfortunately, we too
often disguise ignoble means with noble goals. We do not recognize what we are doing, for the good in all of us—honesty,
compassion, courtesy—gets confused with the desire to get reelected, the need to send a son or daughter to college, excessive
pride, the longing for revenge, the not-so-subtle temptation to
say or do what will get publicity. These, and a host of other
entanglements of the spirit, too often crowd out those better
qualities in us. Then we need to step back and look at ourselves
and our society and recognize the moral struggles we all face.

Stepping back is important to the public official. It provides
some sense of perspective, of what life is all about, and of both
the importance and the insignificance of many of the things we
do. Part of getting a sense of perspective is simply listening.
Lincoln Steffens wrote of Theodore Roosevelt what might be
said of many of us: "It was hard to tell him anything; it was easy
to make him talk, even about a state secret, but to reverse the
process and make him listen was well-nigh impossible."[6] Listening to those isolated voices of wisdom coming from people who
may never see their name in print is part of gaining perspective.
Part of that stepping back includes recognizing the progress that
has been made. What is ethically acceptable is much more strictly
constructed for members of Congress today than fifty or a hundred
years ago. When a secretary of agriculture cracks "jokes" that
degrade the nation's black population, enough people of all ethnic groups feel offended and the secretary must resign. Although
some things improve, others do not. We are not revolted enough
at the indecency of stockpiling weapons of incomprehensible

destructive capability. Attempting to get some perspective on things is important, no matter how inaccurate and unfocused that sense of perspective may be.

The fact that there is a moral struggle within each of us does not mean that we should allow ourselves to become paralyzed. Complexity does not necessarily mean that action is impossible. The goals of peace and justice, of opportunity for employment, of dignity for senior citizens, of conquering cancer and cystic fibrosis—all can be approached even if they are not fully attained. Approaching those goals will not take place if there are no political leaders of vision and courage, two overworked words but underworked realities. "Let the prophet who has a dream tell the dream," the Lord advises Jeremiah.[7] What this nation needs is a dream, a goal, a sense of direction and purpose. Henry Thoreau wrote: "The youth gets together his materials to build a bridge to the moon, or, perchance, a palace or temple on the earth, and, at length, the middle-aged man concludes to build a woodshed with them."[8] There is a danger that our nation is in the middle-age doldrums, that we are planning for woodsheds instead of temples. An old Latin proverb put it differently: "An army of stags led by a lion is more formidable than an army of lions led by a stag."[9] People working with a sense of mission and purpose are more likely to accomplish great things, and less likely to be engaged in activities that harm a society. Such leadership appeals to the best in us, and by that very action restrains somewhat the base and crude and selfish that is in us all. We need more than a woodshed mentality. "My generation lived in preparation for nothing except this war," thirty-two-year-old World War II correspondent Eric Sevareid wrote.[10] We need to feel we are being prepared, not for a war, but for some grander enterprise; even a dull task then takes on new meaning and seems important. That requires leaders who are candid about our limitations, who do not promise too much, who recognize the complexity of the moral decisions that must be made, but at the same time know that we can come closer to understanding other nations and building a solid peace, to reducing poverty in our country and elsewhere, to conquering some of the diseases that plague us. We need leadership that nurtures the sometimes hidden flame of idealism that is a part of all humanity. In an Easter sermon, John Donne said: "All our life is but a going out to the place of execution, to death. Was there ever any man seen to sleep in the cart . . . between the prison and the place of execution? . . . [Yet] we sleep all the way, from the womb to the grave we are never thoroughly awake."[11] We need to be awakened; we need to be lifted.

Representative Wright Patman of Texas was an old-fashioned, courtly member with whom I served. He died at the age of eighty-two while serving in the House. Television crews covering the funeral caught one magnificent line from an old woman who lived in Patman's district: "He rose up mighty high, but he brung us all up with him."

The path upward in politics is a slippery, stumbling one for both the office holder and the public. There are no sure signposts marked with guaranteed success; there are no participants enmeshed solely in virtue. But unless there are those willing to tread the slippery path, willing to stumble, willing to expose themselves, warts and all, willing to give the nation something good and noble toward which to strive, we will follow the downward path—not purposely, but just as certainly as if it were.

"He rose up mighty high, but he brung us all up with him." May some future generation say that of you and me.

Notes

Chapter 1/The Cast of Characters

1. Walt Kelley, *Pogo: We Have Met the Enemy and He Is Us* (New York: Simon and Schuster, 1972).

2. *The Conduct of Life* (1860), p. vi.

3. John E. E. Dalberg-Acton, First Baron Acton, *Essays on Freedom and Power*, edited by Gertrude Himmelfarb (Boston: Beacon Press, 1948), p. 364.

4. Matt. 25:14–30.

5. William Blake, "Auguries of Innocence," lines 97–98, *The Portable Blake* (New York: Viking, 1946), p. 153.

6. Richard John Neuhaus, *Christian Faith and Public Policy* (Minneapolis: Augsburg, 1977), p. 59.

7. Quoted in "An Executive's Inside Look at U.S. Senate," by Albert R. Hunt, *Wall Street Journal*, 16 December 1982, p. 33.

8. "Will and Ariel Durant: Two Authorities of the Past Look Ahead," by James J. Doyle, *Chicago Tribune*, 10 December 1977, p. 11.

9. Source not mentioned, quoted in *History of the Congress* by Alvin M. Josephy (New York: American Heritage, 1975), p. 36.

10. Lincoln Steffens, *The Autobiography of Lincoln Steffens* (New York: Harcourt, Brace, 1937), p. 292.

11. Robert J. Cornell, letter to Paul Simon, 22 March 1983.

12. For more details on the Illinois general assembly in an earlier period see "The Illinois Legislature: A Study in Corruption," by Paul Simon and Alfred Balk, *Harper's*, September 1964, 229:74–78.

13. A tongue-in-cheek statement by Speaker Thomas P. O'Neill in a talk to a group of Democrats, Washington, D.C., 7 February 1978.

14. John Randolph, quoted in *History of the Congress*, by Alvin M. Josephy, Jr. (New York: American Heritage, 1975), p. 131.

15. Quoted by William Bruce, *John Randolph of Roanoke* (New York: Octagon, 1970), 2:39.

16. Hesketh Pearson, *G.B.S.: A Full-length Portrait* (New York: Harper and Brothers, 1942), p. 156.

17. Undated, comment of Joseph Fisher in a Democratic caucus.

18. Plutarch, in *The Great Quotations*, compiled by George Seldes (New York: Lyle Stuart, 1966), p. 570.

Chapter 2/Allen Howe and the People of Utah

1. John Mason Brown, *Through These Men* (1952); quoted in *Scoundrels All*, compiled by Ferdinand Lundesberg (New York: Lyle Stuart, 1968), p. 141.
2. Column, "Congress, Sex and the Press."
3. Aristotle, *Politics*, in *Great Books of the Western World* (Chicago: Encyclopaedia Britannica, 1952), 9:485.
4. Quoted in "Rep. Howe Held on Sex Charge in Utah," *New York Times*, 14 June 1976, p. 23.
5. Editorial, "Howe Should Quit Race as a Service to Utah," *Deseret News*, 15 June 1976, p. A-5.
6. Quoted in "Women and Rights Units Assail Prostitute Decoys," by Horace Lichtenstein, *New York Times*, 16 June 1976.
7. Jim McFarlin, "Arrested Pastor Is Reinstated After 'Almost Unanimous' Vote," *Grand Rapids Press*, 28 May 1977.
8. Quoted in *History of the Presidents*, by the editors of *American Heritage* (New York: American Heritage Publishing, 1968), 2:556.
9. Ibid.
10. Ibid.
11. George F. Will, *The Pursuit of Virtue and Other Tory Notions* (New York: Simon and Schuster, 1982), p. 33.
12. Author unknown. A poem frequently recited by Representative Emanuel Celler, a member of the House from 1923 to 1973.

Chapter 3/Two and Two Sometimes Equal Five

1. Little Buttercup in W. S. Gilbert's *H.M.S. Pinafore* (1878), act 2.
2. P. S 1752.
3. To Gavin Hamilton, quoted by H. L. Mencken, *A Dictionary of American Quotations* (New York: Knopf, 1966), p. 811.
4. *Congressional Record*, 12 May 1977, p. H 14489.
5. Ultimately the tobacco interests prevailed. The Senate did not accept the Johnson amendment, and when the same amendment came up some months later on the omnibus farm bill, the tobacco interests prevailed in the House. The only one of the twenty-eight House members with substantial tobacco to vote with Johnson this time was Charles Bennett of Florida. Of the seventy-one members with smaller amounts of tobacco in their districts, the only members to support the Johnson position were Willis Gradison and Clarence Brown of Ohio, Martha Keys of Kansas, and Richard Ichord of Missouri.
6. Jerry Voorhis, *The Christian in Politics* (New York: Association Press, 1951), p. 100.

7. Elihu Root, quoted by Phillip C. Jessup, "Ethics and Foreign Policy," paper delivered at the University of Virginia, June 1977, p. 3.

8. House debate on HR 5262, Conference Report on Multilaterals, *Congressional Record*, 6 April 1977.

9. Daniel P. Moynihan, "The Politics of Human Rights," *Commentary*, August 1977.

10. Editorial, "Human Rights and Foreign Aid," *Chicago Tribune*, 19 July 1977.

11. Herman Badillo, Thomas Harkin, letter to all members of the House, 10 September 1977.

12. *Public Papers and Addresses of Franklin D. Roosevelt* (New York: Harper and Brothers, 1950), 1944–45 volume, p. 498.

13. Archibald MacLeish, "An Essay on the Founding Ideals and How They Fare Today," *New York Times*, 30 May 1960, p. 14.

Chapter 4/Money

1. Carl Sandburg, interview with Thomas B. Littlewood, quoted in Littlewood's book, *Horner of Illinois* (Northwestern University Press: Evanston, 1969), p. 238.

2. Elizabeth Drew, "Politics and Money—I," *New Yorker*, 6 December 1982, pp. 54–55.

3. Frank McKinney Hubbard, quoted in *Peter's Quotations*, by Dr. Laurence J. Peter (New York: William Morrow, 1977), p. 338.

4. Earl Long, quoted by A. J. Liebling, *The Earl of Louisiana* (Baton Rouge: Louisiana State University Press, 1970), p. 146.

5. H. L. Mencken, quoted by Michael Kilian and Arnold Sawislak, *Who Runs Washington?* (New York: St. Martin's Press, 1982), p. 141.

6. *New Republic* 187, no. 23 (13 December 1982).

7. Will Rogers, newspaper column, 28 June 1931.

8. Justin Dart, quoted by Elizabeth Drew, "Politics and Money—I," *New Yorker*, 6 December 1982, p. 130.

9. Millicent Fenwick, "In Congress: Buy Your Seat or Sell Your Vote," *Washington Post*, 9 November 1982.

10. Arthur Young, quoted by Barbara Ward, *Faith and Freedom* (New York: Norton, 1954), p. 131.

11. Dick Gregory, quoted in *Congressional Record* by William L. Hungate, 13 May 1976, p. E 2562.

12. Sir Thomas More, *Utopia* (New York: E. P. Dutton, 1942), p. 112.

13. Paul Douglas, *In the Fullness of Time* (New York: Harcourt, Brace, Jovanovich, 1971), p. 180.

14. Terry Dolan, quoted in *Holy Terror*, by Flo Conway and Jim Siegelman (Garden City, N.Y.: Doubleday, 1982), p. 98.

15. Louis Harris, "Alienation," *The Harris Survey* 14 (18 February 1982).

16. Oscar Ameringer, *The American Guardian*, quoted in *Scoundrels All*, compiled by Ferdinand Lundberg (New York: Lyle Stuart, 1968), p. 138.

17. Lee Atwater, quoted by Elizabeth Drew, "Politics and Money—I," *New Yorker*, 6 December 1982, p. 68.

18. Ibid., p. 105.

19. George Washington, quoted by Eugene H. Roseboom, *A History of Presidential Elections* (New York: Macmillan, 1959), p. 4.

20. Berkley Bedell, conversation with Paul Simon, 1 March 1983.

21. Walter Isaacson, "Lame Ducks Lay an Egg," *Time* 120, no. 26 (27 December 1982): 13.

22. *Congressional Record*, 14 December 1982, p. H 9718.

23. George McGovern, *Grassroots* (New York: Random House, 1977), p. 8.

24. Jerry Voorhis, Sr., *Confession of Faith* (New York: Vantage Press, 1978), p. 4.

25. Reinhold Niebuhr, quoted by Jerry Voorhis, *Confession of Faith* (New York: Vantage Press, 1978), p. 83.

Chapter 5/The Dilemma of Time

1. Quoted in *Syntopicon of Great Books of the Western World* (Chicago: Encyclopaedia Britannica, 1952), 2:897.

2. Act 5, scene 5, line 49.

3. Speech in New York City, 6 December 1961, *Public Papers of John F. Kennedy* (Washington: National Archives, 1961), p. 497.

4. Jerry Voorhis, letter to Paul Simon, 9 March 1983.

5. Edward Gibbon, *Decline and Fall of the Roman Empire*, in *Great Books of the Western World* (Chicago: Encyclopaedia Britannica, 1952), 41:339.

6. Herodotus, *History*, in *Great Books of the Western World* (Chicago: Encyclopaedia Britannica, 1952), 6:77.

7. Conversation with Paul Simon in 1956.

8. Alfred, Lord Tennyson, "The Last Tournament," *Idylls of the King* (London: Nonesuch Press, 1968), p. 326.

9. *Six Crises* (New York: Doubleday, 1962), p. xvi.

10. Elizabeth Drew, "Politics and Money—I," *New Yorker*, 6 December 1982, p. 149.

11. John Stuart Mill, *Utilitarianism*, in *Great Books of the Western World* (Chicago: Encyclopaedia Britannica, 1952), 43:449.

12. Peter Maurin, quoted by William J. Byron, S.J., president of the Catholic University of America, in an undated paper, "The Meaning of Ethics in Business," p. 5.

13. Act 2, scene 3 of *Othello*.

14. Will Durant, *The Reformation* (New York: Simon and Schuster, 1957), p. 190.

15. Thomas Parnell, "An Elegy to an Old Beauty," line 35, *Poetical Works of Thomas Parnell* (Freeport, N.Y.: Books for Libraries, 1972), pp. 80–82.

16. *Dialogues of Plato, Laws*, Book IV, in *Great Books of the Western World* (Chicago: Encyclopaedia Britannica, 1952), 7:682.

Chapter 6/Inappropriate Responses to World Hunger and the Nuclear Threat

1. Bob Dylan, "Song to Woody," *Writings and Drawings* (New York: Knopf, 1973), p. 5.

2. Address to the United Nations General Assembly, *Public Papers, John F. Kennedy* (Washington: National Archives, 1961), p. 620.

3. Reinhold Niebuhr, *Moral Man and Immoral Society* (New York: Scribner's, 1932), p. 20.

4. Henry Taylor, *Statesman*, quoted in Hans J. Morgenthau, *Dilemmas of Politics* (Chicago: University of Chicago Press, 1958), p. 285.

5. Conversation with the author by a veteran from Edwardsville, Illinois.

6. Some educators favored it from the start, particularly prominent among them the nonpublic school groups who saw it as a means for some limited assistance that would not violate church-state sensitivities.

7. Dr. John Hannah, speaking to a breakfast of Members of Congress for Peace Through Law, July 1976.

8. Jonathan Schell, *The Fate of the Earth* (New York: Knopf, 1982), p. 4.

9. Ruth Ligar Sivard, *World Military and Social Expenditures, 1982* (Leesburg, Va.: World Priorities, 1982), p. 5.

10. Hyman G. Rickover, ibid, p. 7.

11. Ronald Reagan, President's News Conference of 29 January 1981, *Weekly Compilation of Presidential Documents* 17, no. 5. (2 February 1981): 65–66.

12. Ronald Reagan, speech to the National Association of Evangelicals, 8 March 1983, *Presidential Documents* 19, no. 10 (14 March 1983): 369.

13. Saint Augustine, quoted by William Sloane Coffin, "William Sloane Coffin at Gettysburg," *Leaven*, a publication of Gettysburg (Pa.) College, December 1982, p. 4.

14. Henry Steele Commager, quoted by Albert J. Menendez, "The Right Rev. Ronald Reagan," *Church and State* 36, no. 5 (May 1983): 16.

15. Will Durant, *The Reformation* (New York: Simon and Schuster, 1957), p. 113.

16. Study by Roberta Snow, quoted by columnist Ellen Goodman, "Children and the Nuclear Monster," *Washington Post*, 19 February 1983, p. A-23.

17. J. Robert Oppenheimer, quoted by L. Bruce van Voorst, "The Churches and Nuclear Deterrence," *Foreign Affairs*, Spring 1983, p. 828.

18. J. Bryan Hehir, "The Relationship of Moral and Strategic Arguments in the Defense Debate," a paper prepared for the American Political Science Convention, New York City, 31 August 1978, p. 25.

19. Erwin Hargrove, quoted by James M. Wall, unpublished address, "Relating Religion to Politics: Three Modern Modes," 18 March 1983, p. 1.

20. Barbara W. Tuchman, "A Symposium: The Bishops and the Arms Race," *New York Times*, 26 December 1982, p. E-3.

21. "A *Newsweek* Poll: Arms Wrestling," *Newsweek*, 31 January 1983, p. 17.

22. Learned Hand, "The Spirit of Liberty," 21 May 1944, quoted in *The Spirit of Liberty: Papers and Addresses by Learned Hand*, edited by Irving Dilliard (New York: Knopf, 1960), p. 190.

23. Berkley Bedell, note to Paul Simon, 1 March 1983.

Chapter 7/Abortion

1. Magda Denes, "The Abortion Decision: A Case of Moral Myopia," *New Times*, 5 August 1977, p. 17.

2. Daniel Callahan, "Abortion: A Clash of Symbols," chapter in *Moral Choices in Contemporary Society*, edited by Philip Rieff (Del Mar, Calif.: Publishers, Inc.: 1977), p. 13.

3. Linda Bird Francke, *The Ambivalence of Abortion* (New York: Random House, 1978), p. 9.

4. Quoted by Will Durant, *The Life of Greece* (New York: Simon and Schuster, 1966), p. 117.

5. Martin Luther, quoted by Linda Bird Francke, *The Ambivalence of Abortion*, p. 15.

6. Quoted by H. L. Mencken, *A New Dictionary of Quotations* (New York: Knopf, 1966), p. 4.

7. Exod. 21:22, Berkeley Version.

8. *Congregationalist and Boston Recorder*, quoted in James C. Mohr, *Abortion in America* (New York: Oxford University Press, 1978), p. 187.

9. "Pastoral Letter of the Most Reverend Archbishop and Suffragen Prelates of the Province of Baltimore," *Morning Star and Catholic Messenger*, New Orleans, 23 May 1869.

10. *Harris v. McRae*, U.S. Supreme Court, 1980.

11. Quoted in *Holy Terror* by Flo Conway and Jim Siegleman (Garden City, N.Y.: Doubleday, 1982), p. 111.

12. Linda Bird Francke, *The Ambivalence of Abortion*, p. 255.

Chapter 8/Religion

1. Benjamin Whichcote, *Moral and Religious Aphorisms*, 1753.

2. Phillipe Maury, *Politics and Evangelism* (New York: Doubleday, 1959), p. 79.

3. Napoleon I, letter to Count Antoine Thibaudeau, June 1801, quoted by H. L. Mencken, *A New Dictionary of Quotations* (New York: Knopf, 1942), p. 1018.

4. Henry Fairlie, "The Perils of Political Prayers," *Washington Post*, 23 May 1976, p. C-1.

5. Ibid.

6. Jerry Voorhis, *The Christian in Politics* (New York: Association Press, 1951), p. 3.

7. Will Durant, *The Reformation* (New York: Simon and Schuster, 1957), p. 4.

8. Reinhold Niebuhr, quoted by June Bingham, *Courageto Change* (New York: Scribner's, 1961), p. 8.

9. Peter L. Benson and Dorothy L. Williams, *Religion on Capitol Hill: Myths and Realities* (San Francisco: Harper and Row, 1982), p. ix.

10. Tom Wicker, "In the Nation: Wallace's Powerful Medicine," *New York Times,* 12 December 1967.

11. *Official Report of the Fifth Baptist World Congress,* quoted by William Lloyd Allen, "How Baptists Assessed Hitler," *Christian Century* 99, no. 27 (1–8 September 1982): 890.

12. Dr. John R. Sampey, quoted by William Lloyd Allen, "How Baptists Assessed Hitler," *Christian Century* 99, no. 27 (1–8 September 1982): 890.

13. John W. Bradbury, writing for the *Watchman-Examiner,* 13 September 1934, quoted by William Lloyd Allen, "How Baptists . . ."

14. Dr. Charles Leek, *Alabama Baptist,* 6 September 1934, quoted by William Lloyd Allen, "How Baptists . . . ,"

15. Frank Buchman, quoted by June Bingham, *Courage to Change* (New York: Scribner's, 1961), p. 202.

16. Ronald Reagan, speech to the National Association of Evangelicals, 8 March 1983, *Presidential Documents* 19, no. 10 (14 March 1983): 369.

17. Quoted in *Religion on Capitol Hill: Myths and Realities* by Peter L. Benson and Dorothy L. Williams (San Francisco: Harper and Row, 1982), p. 172.

18. "Open Letter From Jerry Falwell," advertisement of the Moral Majority, *Washington Post,* 7 March 1983, p. A-26.

19. Lance Morrow, "To Revive Responsibility," *Time* 117, no. 8 (23 February 1981): 74.

20. Undated four-page folder, distributed 31 October 1982. Christian Voice Moral Government Fund, Washington, D.C.

21. Acts 12:22.

22. Jim Wright, "Legislation and the Will of God," in *Congress and Conscience,* edited by John B. Anderson (Philadelphia: Lippincott, 1970), p. 33.

23. Cromwell, Letter to the General Assembly of the Church of Scotland, 3 August 1650, *Writings and Speeches of Oliver Cromwell* (New York: Russell and Russell, 1970), 2:303.

24. Peter L. Berger, "The Class Struggle in American Religion," *Christian Century,* 25 February 1981.

25. Quoted by Barbara Ward, *Faith and Freedom* (New York: W. W. Norton, 1954), p. 65.

26. Quoted by Carl S. Meyer, "Development of the American Pattern in Church-State Relations," *Church and State Under God,* edited by Albert G. Huegli (St. Louis: Concordia, 1964), p. 202.

27. Ibid., p. 203.

28. Will Durant, *The Reformation* (New York: Simon and Schuster, 1957), p. 212.

29. William McKinley, "First Annual Message to the Senate and House of Representatives, December 6, 1897," in *A Compilation of the Messages and Papers of the Presidents,* prepared under the direction of the Joint Committee on Printing of the House and Senate (New York: Bureau of National Literature, Inc., 1930), 13:6258–63.

30. Quoted by Reinhold Niebuhr, *Moral Man and Immoral Society* (New York: Scribner's, 1932), p. 99.

31. Donald G. Jones and Russell E. Richey, "A Harmonizing of Moral Claims," *Christian Century,* January 5–12, 1977, p. 5.

32. Rosemary Ruether, "Mystification of Liberation," *Christian Century,* 5–12 January 1977, p. 4.

33. Hans J. Morgenthau, *Dilemmas of Politics* (Chicago: University of Chicago Press, 1958), p. 249.

34. Martin E. Marty, *The Public Church* (New York: Crossroad, 1981), p. 13.

35. Dr. Rita Swan, letter to Representative Berkley Bedell, 12 November 1982, p. 1.

36. Ibid., p. 5.

37. Jim Quinn, "Kosciusko Child Fights for Life as Church Controversy Flares," *Fort Wayne News-Sentinel,* 20 November 1982.

38. James M. Wall, unpublished address, "Relating Religion to Politics: Three Modern Modes," p. 3.

39. Walter Lippmann, *A Preface to Morals* (New York: Macmillan, 1929), p. 8.

40. Phillipe Maury, *Evangelism and Politics* (New York: Doubleday, 1959), p. 75,

41. Martin E. Marty, "Commencement Address [Christ Seminary, St. Louis]," quoted in *Together* 5, no. 4 (June-July 1979): 8.

Chapter 9/The Political Parties

1. Sir Joseph Porter in W. S. Gilbert's *H.M.S. Pinafore* (1878), act 1.

2. Aristotle, *Politics,* Book V, in *Great Books of the Western World* (Chicago: Encyclopaedia Britannica, 1951), 9:512.

3. James Boswell, *Life of Samuel Johnson LL.D.,* in *Great Books of the Western World* (Chicago: Encyclopaedia Britannica, 1952), 44:260.

4. "A Conversation with George F. Kennan," by George Urban, *Encounter,* September 1976, p. 14.

5. Niccolò Machiavelli, *The Prince,* in *Great Books of the Western World* (Chicago: Encyclopaedia Britannica, 1952), 23:14.

6. Henry Jones Ford, *The Rise and Growth of American Politics* (New York: Macmillan, 1898), pp. 239–40.

7. Theodore H. White, "Weinberger on the Ramparts," *New York Times Magazine*, 6 February 1983, p. 77.

8. William Graham Summer, in *The Challenge of Facts and Other Essays*, edited by A. G. Keller (New Haven: Yale University Press, 1914), p. 367.

9. Austin Ranney, *The Doctrine of Responsible Party Government* (Urbana: University of Illinois Press, 1954), p. 21.

10. Woodrow Wilson, *Congressional Government* (Boston: Houghton Mifflin, 1885), p. 93.

11. Woodrow Wilson, "Government Under the Constitution," in *An Old Master, and Other Political Essays* (New York: Scribner's, 1893), pp. 31–33, 91–96.

12. Gillis Long, Proceedings of the Democratic Caucus of the House of Representatives, 16 September 1981, p. 5. Use of this material from the caucus is with the permission of the caucus and the individuals quoted.

13. Ibid, p. 6.

14. Ibid, p. 18.

15. Ibid, p. 98.

16. Ibid, p. 25.

17. Ibid, pp. 37–38.

18. Jerry Voorhis, *The Christian in Politics* (New York: Association Press, 1951), p. 24.

19. John Rhodes, *The Futile System* (Garden City, N.Y.: EPM Publications, 1976), p. 7.

20. Rutherford B. Hayes, Inaugural Address, 5 March 1877.

Chapter 10/Balancing Self-restraint and Leadership

1. Studs Terkel, *Talking to Myself* (New York: Pantheon Books, 1973), p. 66.

2. Phillip Rieff, "The Nature of Morality," *Moral Choices in Contemporary Society* (San Diego: Publishers Inc., 1976), p. 4.

3. Sir Thomas More, quoted in *The Utopia of Sir Thomas More*, notes and introduction by Mildred Campbell (New York: Walter J. Black, 1947), p. 247.

4. Quoted by Haynes Johnson, "The Most Unhappy Talk of This Town," *Washington Post*, 17 July 1977.

5. Will and Ariel Durant, *The Lessons of History* (New York: Simon and Schuster, 1968), p. 30.

6. Jerald C. Brauer, "The Rule of the Saints in American Politics," *Church History* (September 1958), 27:240.

7. Charles Sumner, quoted by Vic Fredericks, *The Wit and Wisdom of Presidents* (New York: F. Fell, 1966), p. 161.

8. I. F. Stone to about twelve House members at an informal meeting that included the author, January 1975.

9. Les AuCoin, quoted by James M. Naughton, "The Lost Innocence of Congressman AuCoin," *New York Times*, 31 August 1975.

10. Source for the saying is unknown. Used occasionally by James Choissier, editor of the *Benton* (Illinois) *Evening News* in his column, "Odds and Ends."

11. Mother Jones, quoted in *Mother Jones, the Miners' Angel* by Dale Fetherling (Carbondale, Ill.: Southern Illinois University Press, 1974), p. 192.

12. Ibid, p. 85.

13. Will Durant, *The Reformation* (New York: Simon and Schuster, 1957), p. 145.

14. Laotse, *The Wisdom of Laotse*, translated by Lin Yutang (New York: Modern Library, 1948), p. 114.

15. John F. Kennedy, quoted by Kenneth P. O'Donnell, a member of his staff, "With Your Guns and Drums . . . ," *New York Times*, 22 November 1972, p. 35.

16. Alexis de Tocqueville, *Democracy in America* (New York: Vintage Books, 1954), 2:236.

Chapter 11/The God of Public Opinion

1. Albert Gore, Sr., *Let the Glory Out* (New York: Viking, 1972), p. 6.

2. J. William Fulbright, "The Legislator as Educator," *Foreign Affairs*, Spring 1979, p. 722.

3. James H. Boren in *Peter's Quotations* by Laurence J. Peter (New York: Morrow, 1977), p. 296.

4. Pascal, *Pensées*, in *Great Books of the Western World* (Chicago: Encyclopaedia Britannica, 1952), 33:345.

5. Plato, *The Republic*, Book IV, in *Great Books of the Western World* (Chicago: Encyclopaedia Britannica, 1952), 7:378.

6. A. Lawrence Lowell, quoted by Austin Ranney, *The Doctrine of Responsible Party Government* (Urbana: University of Illinois Press, 1954), p. 50.

7. John Stuart Mill, *On Liberty* (1859), in *Great Books of the Western World* (Chicago: Encyclopaedia Britannica, 1952), 43:299.

8. Plutarch, *The Lives of the Noble Grecians and Romans* (Dryden translation), in *Great Books of the Western World* (Chicago: Encyclopaedia Britannica, 1952), 14:648–49.

9. Cicero, quoted in *Scoundrels All*, compiled by Ferdinand Lundberg (New York: Lyle Stuart, 1968), p. 27.

10. Joseph H. Ball, quoted in *Scoundrels All*, compiled by Ferdinand Lundberg (New York: Lyle Stuart, 1968), p. 88.

Chapter 12/The Media

1. Attributed, rightly or wrongly, to a St. Louis judge.

2. Resolution of the Northwest Conference of the Methodist Episcopal Church, adopted at Lafayette, Indiana, 24 June 1933, quoted by H. L. Mencken, *A New Dictionary of Quotations* (New York: Knopf, 1966), p. 852.

3. Daniel Schorr, *Clearing the Air* (Boston: Houghton Mifflin, 1977), p. 294.

4. David Obey, prepared remarks for the Western Wisconsin Press Association, Eau Claire, Wisconsin, 27 May 1977, p. 2.

5. Jim Wright, "Legislation and the Will of God," *Congress and Conscience,* edited by John B. Anderson (Philadelphia: Lippincott, 1970), p. 31.

6. Isa. 16:11.

7. Conversation with Paul Simon, 11 February 1983.

8. John Naisbitt, *Megatrends* (New York: Warner Books, 1982), p. 60.

9. *St. Louis Globe-Democrat,* 13 September 1976, p. 3A.

10. Hodding Carter, "Inside Story" television series, Public Television, 7 April 1983.

11. Adlai E. Stevenson, interview by Barbara Reynolds, *USA Today,* 25 March 1983, p. 11A.

12. Irving Dilliard, "The Editor I Wish I Were," *The Responsibility of the Press,* edited by Gerald Gross (New York: Simon and Schuster, 1966), p. 125.

13. Fred Starr, "Needed: A Cure for Provincialism," *Chronicle of Higher Education,* 8 March 1976.

14. Frank Lloyd Wright, quoted in *Peter's Quotations,* by Dr. Laurence J. Peter (New York: William Morrow, 1977), p. 323.

15. H. L. Mencken to Paul Patterson, 21 July 1928, in "Newspapers, Women and Beer: The Letters of H. L. Mencken," *Harper's* 253, no. 1516 (September 1976): 47.

16. Advice of a senior executive of a newspaper chain, quoted by John McCormally, editor of the *Burlington* (Iowa) *Hawk Eye* in a speech to the University of Iowa School of Journalism.

17. Allen Neuharth of Gannett Newspapers, quoted by Robert D. Reid, "Can't Edit a Good Newspaper with an Accountant's Heart," *Southern Illinoisan,* 6 February 1983, p. 18.

18. Oron J. Hale, *The Captive Press in the Third Reich* (Princeton: Princeton University Press, 1964), p. 5.

19. Daniel Schorr, *Clearing the Air* (Boston: Houghton Mifflin, 1977), p. 287.

20. William Randolph Hearst, quoted by James Creelman, *On the Great Highway* (Boston: Lothrop, 1901), p. 178.

21. *New York Journal and Advertiser,* 18 February 1898.

22. J. Fenimore Cooper, *The American Democrat* (New York: Knopf, 1981), p. 156.

Chapter 13/Conclusion

1. Oliver Wendell Holmes, quoted in *Morality and Foreign Policy* by Kenneth W. Thompson (Baton Rouge: Louisiana State University Press, 1980), p. 71.

2. Judith Exner, quoted in "Judith Campbell Exner" by Sally Quinn, *Washington Post,* 24 June 1977, p. B-3.

3. George Will, "Clouding Salvador Issues," *Chicago Sun-Times,* 13 March 1983, p. 8 of Viewpoint Section.

4. Television commercial, Channel 3, Harrisburg, Illinois, 18 January 1983.

5. Kenneth W. Thompson, "Ethics and Responsibility in the Political Arena: An Overview," in *Ethics and Government*, Annual Chief Justice Earl Warren Conference on Advocacy in the United States (Washington: Roscoe Pound-American Trial Lawyers Foundation, 1982), p. 81.

6. Lincoln Steffens, *The Autobiography of Lincoln Steffens* (New York: Harcourt, Brace, 1931), p. 31.

7. Jer. 23:28.

8. Henry Thoreau, *Journal* 14 (New York: Dover, 1962), 14 July 1852 entry.

9. Plutarch, *Chabriae Apophtegmata*, as quoted in *The Macmillan Book of Proverbs*, edited by Burton Stevens (New York: Macmillan, 1948), p. 1373.

10. Eric Sevareid, *Not So Wild a Dream* (New York: Atheneum, 1976).

11. *The Complete Poetry and Selected Prose of John Donne*, introduction by Robert Hillyer (New York: Random House, 1941), p. 385.

Index